Home Smart Home

T0326705

for Annette

Home Smart Home
How We Want to Live

Oliver Herwig

Birkhäuser
Basel

What counts in a smart home?

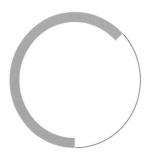

User-friendliness
63 %

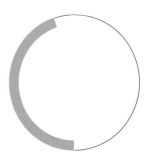

Cost-effectiveness
45 %

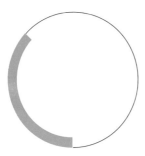

Data security and protection
37 %

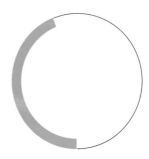

Good test results
44 %

Voice control
22 %

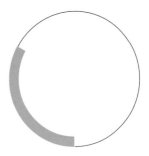

Compatibility
33 %

The Hybrid Home:
The Apartment Search

The Apartment Search

"Oh yes, I'd like that:
A villa in a natural setting with a big terrace,
The Baltic in front, Friedrichstraße at the rear,
With a lovely view, bucolic-chic,
And the Zugspitze visible from the bathroom –
But in the evenings, it's not far to the cinema."

Kurt Tucholsky,
The Ideal,
1927

In its marvelous exorbitance, Tucholsky's "ideal"[1] is astonishingly contemporary. Nearly a century after its publication, the housing question once again marks the fault line of a society in a state of change. Our lives are more cosmopolitan and more individual, more diverse and more accelerated than ever before. Small wonder, then, that so much has become blurred: spaces and perceptions, dreams and certainties. Long-separated aspects of life unexpectedly converge: work and leisure, public and private. Rooms become spaces where contradictory expectations collide. We operate a busy home office while yearning for the amenities of a hotel. And while the world outside spills over into our own four walls, while we efface our own boundaries medially, we are forced to adapt to the constraints of outdated layouts and limited space.[2]

Welcome to the hybrid home, which dissolves the monofunctional room, together with its rituals – think of the shared TV evening – for which it was reserved for so long. Forms of residence are changing. Emerging today are spaces without clear designations, living-kitchen-workspaces that resemble an Italian restaurant at one moment, a fan block in a divided soccer stadium at another, a place to do homework at yet another. The reasons for this metamorphosis are numerous, but are for the most part financial: rising rents[3] compel city dwellers to downsize, to use fewer square meters more efficiently. Whether voluntarily or of necessity, more and more people are trying out residential communities for adults.[4] This need not necessarily be coliving, a variant of coworking, which involves sharing an apartment between shifting groups for scheduled time periods: many people value communal life together with options for personal retreat, open-living kitchens, and flexible guest rooms where one-half of an oversized sofa is parked on the balcony.

Our conceptions of dwelling have become unstable. Yet again. At one time, modernity promised progress through hygiene – and set standards such as running water, central heating, kitchenettes, and bathrooms. In 1927 this project was embodied by the Werkbundsiedlung (Werkbund Housing

The Apartment Search

Estate) in Stuttgart. Ludwig Mies van der Rohe promoted the idea that "a new form of dwelling has an impact beyond four walls."[5] Residential development and lifestyles were expressions and catalysts of societal modernization. To cite Mies van der Rohe's opening address at the building exhibition: "The struggle for a new form of housing (is) only one aspect of the larger struggle for new ways of living." Mies made it clear that the "problem of the new housing" resided in the "altered material, social, and intellectual structure" of the time. Today, we can make similar arguments, although the challenges of the twenty-first century assume new dimensions: climate change and digital disruption. But something else as well links the 1920s with the 2020s: housing shortages. The developers of Red Vienna and the New Frankfurt confronted housing shortages through cost-efficient building, and those of the Weißenhofsiedlung[6] experimented with skeleton structures and prefabrication, while contemporary architects are actively testing modular systems, factory prefabrication, and digital building processes. They also strive to conceive their projects in an energy-efficient, sustainable, recyclable, and systemic fashion (cradle-to-cradle).

Contemporary housing development is obliged to accommodate antagonistic utilizations and needs within a restricted space: relationships and work, family, school, and friends – with the mobile device as the central control unit of the smart home. Walls lined with books and CD collections are replaced now with online offerings, while the progressive digitalization extends beyond the dematerialization of objects: concepts such as inner and outer, work and leisure, self and world swirl together confusingly. Altered as a consequence is the balance between privacy, intimacy, and public life – along with the ways in which we present ourselves medially.

From a sociological perspective, modern residence rests on four pillars: socially as the location of the bigenerational family; functionally as a place of leisure and reproduction; in terms of social psychology, as a sphere of intimacy; and economically, as a purchasable or leasable commodity.[7] Today, only the last of these pillars remains standing: the dwelling takes the form of real estate. Everything else is in a state of flux. Nor is this upheaval the result of chance. Mirrored in the boundaryless home is a boundaryless society, which introduces flexible work and thinking around the clock (24/7) into a home where the family no longer resembles any standard model, and the private, even the intimate, becomes broadcastable. Rooms must become multifunctional, transformed into chameleon-style zones – or are threatened with obsolescence.

But there remains hope as well – as soon as we abandon the living cell and conceive of the city as an expanded living room.[8] Now, life takes place outside, in the cafe, on the park bench, and on the street, which is slowly being liberated from the dominance of automobile traffic and reserved parking zones – or instead in the expanses of the Web and social media. Whoever lives in a small residential unit (or as we say today, a micro-apartment) must necessarily become more open. Flexible supplemental space is in demand: collective residential amenities, shared party kitchens and roof terraces that are readily adaptable to individual needs. Emerging now is genuine networking, encounters between neighbors who otherwise have little more contact than occasionally receiving packages for one another. This can engender a sense of community, and even friendship. Everything else is digital.

The Apartment Search

More and more people are using smart home applications

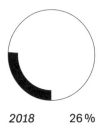

2018   26 %

2019   31 %

2020   37 %

16 – 29 years of age
43 %

30 – 49 years of age
45 %

50 – 64 years of age
49 %

Starting at 65 years of age
13 %

The Apartment Search

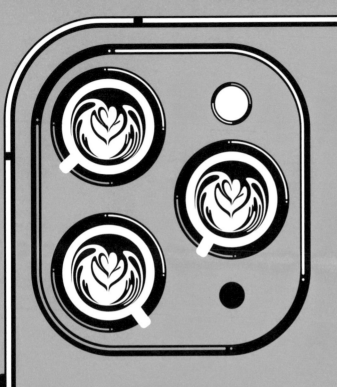

Privacy Was Yesterday:
The Instagram Apartment

For most people, decluttering is a far from easy task. Today, however, it is obligatory for anyone who wants to project a positive image on social networks. Who wants to display a messy room, a vase of wilted flowers, underwear, or dust bunnies behind a half-opened door? The more images of seemingly perfect apartments stream through our visual field, the more interior décor becomes a moral issue. Platforms like Instagram and Pinterest condition our expectations about how things should look. Bright, tidy, design-heavy, and with a certain je ne sais quois that distinguishes us, hopefully, from everyone else. The undiminished importance of "cultural distinction" was clarified recently by a study that was summarized by Boris Holzer as follows: currently, the aim is to maintain an openness to "various forms of cultural production" while to some extent, at the same time, tossing the separation between "high" and "low" overboard. The trivial stands alongside the discerning, while discursively, it is important to specify the correct categories, for example with television series such as "Breaking Bad" and "Mad Men."[9] Distinction operates through the correct codes.

Everyone joins in. Meanwhile, a similar effect is manifest with highly-processed images of stars and celebrities whose optimized appearance often makes ordinary mortals look simply old, kindling a desire for drastic cosmetic adjustments. Suddenly, all we see are corners we would prefer not to post online. Those who must constantly measure themselves against the self-staging of others will either become experts at decluttering and interior design, or instead mired in a permanent PR crisis. Has the table been wiped? The trash disposed of? Has the picture been straightened? Since, according to a current study by the MaLisa Stiftung, 71% of women active on YouTube display themselves in their own apartments,[10] the portals have opened directly onto human interiors. This goes beyond styling or a few casually dispersed coffee-table books, to say nothing of Christmas decorations, which are expected to bring joy to all.[11] All of which resembles a creative mission with constant success monitoring via the Internet, which is meanwhile used "at least occasionally"[12] by 94% of the German-speaking population aged 14 or older. As a

The Apartment Search

rule, comparison does not bring happiness. Like it or not. "You need a perfect image, and this can require up to 20 attempts, which is just nerve-racking," the study cites an Instagram user as saying. An isolated case? Hardly. A result of collective self-presentation: evidently, we are becoming increasingly homogenous,[13] and we suffer when "likes" are withheld from us.

Not everyone is a born self-promoter. In this respect, much can be learned from professionals like Louis XIV, who conceived Versailles as an open stage upon which he performed as the principal protagonist of his own life – like an inverted forebearer of *The Truman Show*. It hardly seems surprising, then, that the accessories of such costume dramas come to mind again when we employed mirrors and perspective to guide the field of vision into the space during the next videoconference – and then back to us. And it was no coincidence that the Sun King chose the bed chamber as the place to link together his corporeal existence with matters of state. The bed was both a regenerative device as well as the symbolic center of France. It was therefore only logical that the daily morning lever du Roi was celebrated as an act of state, accompanied by pomp and ritual. The stately bed chamber still resonates in John Lennon and Yoko Ono's inspired "Bed-In" performance of 1969 or Beyoncé's bedroom appearance[14] – and of course in the productions of all YouTube specialists. It is a question of coverage and clicks, and sometimes even of viewer ratings. The commingling of private, intimate matters with business is strategic, along with targeted indiscretions, when the reception is right – a societal event, both then and now.

The apartment has long been a mélange of openness to and retreat from the world outside, a shapeshifter that is expected to be everything simultaneously – and no longer exclusively private. We share it with partners, friends, and followers, and at times, even now, with family members. And in any case with the virtual office, a place devoid of time clocks and doors that is potentially active perpetually and everywhere. And at the same time, we willingly expose ourselves via social media.

The private in the literal sense of exclusivity[15] has ceased to exist, and even the basic right to the "inviolability of the private sphere"[16] seems to be at least partially eroded in daily life – more or less voluntarily. MoMA curator Terence Riley anticipated the wretchedness of the digitalized world two decades ago already with the pioneering exhibition *The Un-Private House,*[17] his reflection upon the new culture of self-presentation. Today, we can expand the argument presented in 1999, asserting that the "un-private home" has relinquished the quality that long characterized it: shelter. The home, the domestic sphere, was always bound up with the notion that it was possible to close the door behind you, and hence shut out the world at large (the world of work, of other people) – at least for an evening or a night. The domestic study was more a status symbol than a necessity. This has changed, and fundamentally.

The inner life, the life of the soul, is no longer sharply distinguishable from the world outside – and this is not due solely to the presence of the mobile devices that lie scattered around us, with their tiny display screens and even smaller sensors. We too have changed, along with our attitude toward the possibility of publicly projecting – or posting – private matters, even intimate ones. We tweet, chat, and network ceaselessly. Professionally as well as personally. Nor is it clear any longer where the one ends and the other begins. The Web, with its interfaces, is perpetually present. If we like, we can report live from our bedrooms – at any time of day, and even at night. In screwball comedies, the lovers are continually interrupted by the ringing telephone, and come together only under the most vexing conditions; even during the love act itself, James Bond picks up the receiver when the phone rings. Today, we are all familiar with the situation: the outside can no longer be disconnected; at most, we can disengage briefly and go on standby. The mediatized world eliminates the traditional roles of sender and receiver. We receive and transmit simultaneously, speaking into the tablet while secretly checking to see that all is well – from the wardrobe to the backdrop, the carefully selected fragment of the apartment that continually appears.

The Apartment Search

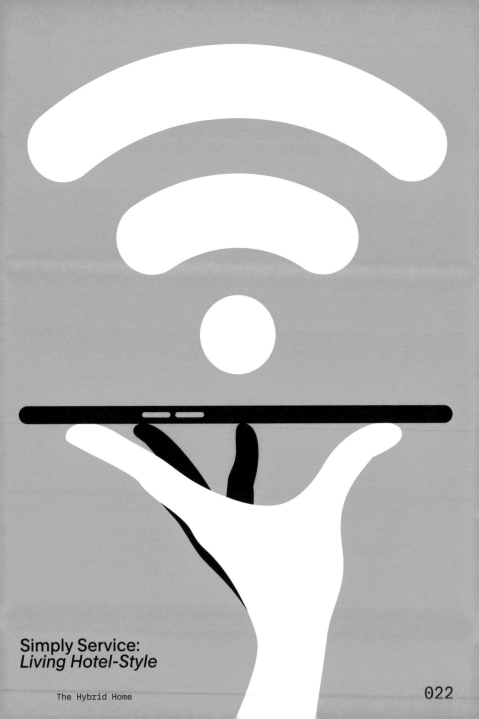

Simply Service:
Living Hotel-Style

It's probably an addiction, even something much worse. We yearn for a modicum of luxury in the fast-paced daily routine of appointments and to-do lists. More convenience, more service. Observable in recent years is the creeping "hotelization"[18] of habitation. Bit by bit, we procure everything we have grown to like in Rio, Rome, and Rimini into our own four walls – objects, but even more so, moods. As different as these home-hotels may appear in detail, three characteristic traits recur: simplicity, which takes the form of an emphatic casualness; maximum comfort, noticeable as a rule only at second glance (with Dolby surround sound even in the bathroom and precision lighting control in the hallway); and unobtrusive service. No one wants the inconvenience of ironing or shopping any longer when these services can be procured at any moment – in the knowledge, however, that our new-won personal freedom is made possible by the dubious working conditions of the new service personnel.[19] In the end, an interior design style becomes a lifestyle, one that is shared in immaculate, consummately staged Insta-posts.

Before COVID and daily videoconferencing, we were perpetually on the go – despite climate change. Whether on business, or just slinging a weekender over one shoulder, it was always: off to the airport. Meanwhile, this sensibility has been carried over into our own four walls. That this occurs is ensured already by the images we post ourselves or discover on platforms. Their constant presence conditions our perceptions of what counts as beautiful or normal. In force earlier was the psychology of acquisition. Vacation experiences were woven into everyday life via souvenirs, images, and plenty of mental cinema.[20] Many people invest in experiences and images, partly because every vacation resonates on social media. An Instagram image here, a breezy Tweet there, and gigabytes of data on cell phones and PCs. Images have become the hardest available status currency. As early as 1999 B. Joseph Pine II and James H. Gilmore had something to say about this "Experience Economy."[21] Their thesis: we purchase moments of happiness because we already own everything else. Preferably while traveling. And Central Europeans have had plenty of practice. The Swiss Office of Federal Statistics reports that in 2019, on average, "each Swiss resident took an average of 2.9 overnight and ten day trips";[22] incidentally, two-thirds of these journeys involve crossing national borders.

On vacations, we are temporarily liberated from our preoccupations and our possessions. There was that bed-and-breakfast with a view of the rocky coastline of – let's say – Polignano a Mare. The sea swell, the cool breeze, the fresh air in a room that consisted of little more than a bed and a tall ceiling. The closet was an improvised corner where the clothes dangled; everything else vanished into a container that merged somehow with the bed. No other furnishings were needed. Things could be this laid-back at home too. The luxury of simplicity, invigorated by a few days at the seashore. In 2014 a study by the Boston Consulting Group discovered that such "luxury experiences" are becoming increasingly important.[23] You just let it melt in your mouth: experiences tend to outdo merchandise, outcompeting the accumulation of commodities. This transformation of values is not necessarily sustainable: novel experiences in the Hindu Kush or a retreat in the outback of Australia can have genuinely negative consequences for the personal life cycle assessment.

One magazine in particular is responsible for the fact that half of the world is now furnished in cocoa and mother-of-pearl: the Wallpaper* style sloshes back from our travels into the living room, together with sophisticated trends and intellectual snapshots. Luxury resorts have long since celebrated natural materials: stone and wood. Then there is the fact that we have always yearned for a look behind the scenes, to live like the Romans when in Rome, ideally in a rented apartment with a view of the Pantheon, including the patina we miss so much in our fast-paced lives, with its promise of deceleration and a sense of permanence. Another path is known as smart simplicity. Even hotel chains demonstrate that you can actually live in the lounge. All that is required is a few classics like Arne Jacobsen's Egg Chair or a comfortable leather sofa landscape with a bar and a good café au lait while your room is being cleaned by service personnel. Round-the-clock service offerings promise a welcome focus on the essential: life itself.

Posed anew with each trip is the question of home and its furnishings: the lightweight, airy feel of vacation days ricochets back onto everyday life – with thin fabrics, lightweight furnishings, bright colors, consummate technology, and elevated expectations when it comes to service. Is the hotel the new standard for upscale interior architecture? Opening up, meanwhile, through a combination of well-designed interiors and impeccable service is a market that blurs the boundaries between the standard old-style hotel room, the ultra-individualized Airbnb, and one's own home. Boardinghouses or serviced apartments, furnished apartments for weekend commuters and temporary employees, frequent flyers and employees en route to the next career assignment, wherever that might be: these options combine the amenities of the hotel (laundry, cleaning, anonymity) with the advantages of the private home. They are regarded as having great potential for growth, concretely: growth rates of up to 48% by 2021.[24] More than half of the more than 6000 firms surveyed by Statista[25] use such units for business trips. A market report by Austria Real regards this as an expression of a "societal transformation": the desire for "flexible, individual, and maximally cost-efficient forms of residence."[26] That this hybrid of hotel and private apartment has been so well-received is no accident: it absolves us of responsibility.

Even more remarkable, however, is the way in which our conception of the home has been altered by constant travel. The corresponding imagery shifts between ostentatious casualness, invisible comfort, and services that can read our desires directly from our gazes. This means round-the-clock service provision of the kind that existed earlier only at Mom's place – without a moralizing undertone, perhaps with butler and chauffeur services. In Hamburg, XING founder Lars Hinrichs built the "Apartimentum," a highly networked living environment for the expats of our time. Hinrichs leases "quality of life by the cubic meter."

The personalized hotel shows how flexible we have become when it comes to home life. And although COVID has decelerated some forms of movement considerably, we still live in different places to an increasing degree. And they may look exactly like a serviced apartment. The main thing is that WLAN reception is good. This is the phenomenon referred to by sociologists as multilocality, meaning that more and more people live in an increasing number of residential locations – and not just an engineer with an apartment in Bern and a workplace in Basel, but also tradespeople from Saxony working on the Berlin-Brandenburg Airport, for example. Willingly or otherwise, we have become more mobile: traditional family structures – father, mother, children – are vanishing. In some metropolises, according to Christine Hannemann of the Institut Wohnen und Entwerfen (Institute of Housing and Design) at Stuttgart University, only 18% of households consist of families. Hannemann's area of expertise is architecture and housing sociology. And although families continue to be valued highly, "the classical nuclear family" demands "only a minimal interval of the life cycle. Given a life span of 96 years, perhaps 25 years."[27] Needless to say, this has consequences: for the way we live, for what is regarded as normal – and desirable.

The Apartment Search

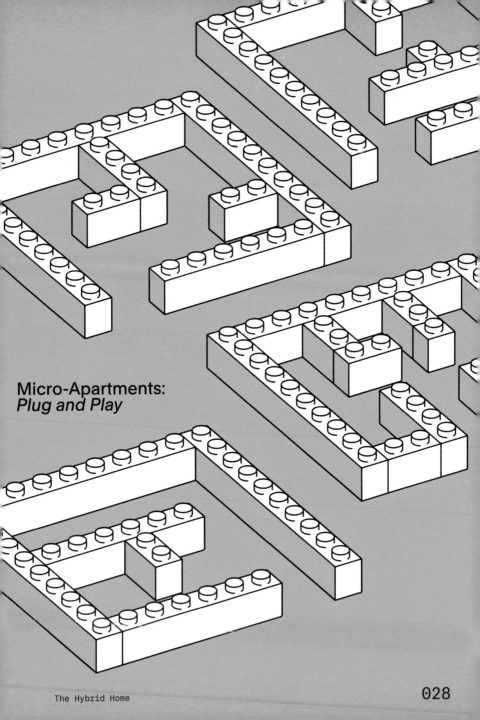

Micro-Apartments:
Plug and Play

In digital modernism, people are expected to adapt themselves flexibly to changing work environments. Small wonder then that even when traveling abroad, we cultivate demands that are conditioned by digital infrastructure: 5G and WLAN, routers and access codes. Living arrangements are no exception, especially when they are condensed into an ultracompact mix of living bathroom and kitchenette. Throw down your bag, locate your socks, unpack your toothbrush – this ritual is not confined to the hotel room. It carries over as well into residential preferences, which aim toward pragmatism and matter-of-factness. No one wants to search for the power outlets. Futurologist Stephan Jung predicts that the members of Generation Y will change jobs circa 17 times, and move house circa 15 times. This means that "relocation and occupation" will need to function according to the "plug and play principal."[28] Every frequent traveler can grasp the implications. No one will need to masquerade as a digital nomad to take part.

But there is something else, something fundamental: density is no abstract sociological concept; we are aware of our neighbors, we hear them, even with doors closed. Which does not mean that new forms of social interaction are on the horizon. Things are getting crowded in the metropolises, and real estate prices are going through the roof. Munich, Hamburg, and Milan, and even Regensburg and Linz are becoming unaffordable. The housing shortage is nothing new, while isolated villages and disconnected rural areas have become orphaned. All of this could be shrugged off as a luxury problem, of course, since overall, we utilize more resources and take up more space than any previous generation.[29] As close as we may seem digitally, we live at a constructed distance from one another. Today, 47 m² are the measure of all things.[30] The "Singles Republic" demands greater constructive expenditures and distance, coinciding with (and this is no contradiction) greater digital openness. In the ascendance today in larger cities is a form of habitation that is reminiscent of our study years: the space-optimized micro-apartment with one-and-a-half to two rooms, kitchen, and bath.[31] Users forego additional square meters in order to live in town, hopefully where the action is. For all age groups, location is the deciding factor. Even so-called silversurfers want to avoid growing old in the suburbs, and prefer living somewhere with options: infrastructure and culture. No apartment is forever. It serves as a flexible, temporary shell. Only one thing matters: the smaller the better, but embedded in the urban fabric.

Whoever comments on housing must also ponder density. Dietrich Fink, a professor at the Technical University Munich, is not alone in perceiving densification as an opportunity for cities.[32] Decisive here are flexible residential units that accommodate as many life plans as possible. Compactness teaches self-discipline. It is striking how many small apartments make such a neat impression: storage space is minimized, yet everything seems so tidy. Immediately upon entry, room-height glazing generates a feeling of spaciousness. With such compact dimensions, of course, it would never occur to anyone to set up a country-style wardrobe. Whatever doesn't fit into the apartment ends up in the basement. Which makes storage space an important criterion. Since there are no balconies, the same is true for common spaces for gatherings, such as roof terraces.

Many co-op buildings are trying out convertible spaces and flexible supplementary offerings that are available to users for delimited time periods. The citizens of the "Singles Republic," with their optimized micro-apartments, are seeking new avenues for establishing contact, for example through common rooms where women and men can cook, work, and hang out together. An option not restricted to young professionals: meanwhile, older people as well swear by the rewards of coworking and coliving. Despite all of the euphoria about new forms of cohabitation, micro-apartments themselves remain a design challenge, an example being the configuration of access to the numerous units. Who is enthusiastic about balcony access apartments? And in many cases, front-to-back floor plans are no longer possible. In addition, energy-optimized apartments often necessitate a back-to-back alignment. A quality micro-apartment reveals itself through its layout, which however must be as flexible as possible: why shouldn't three micro-apartments become a two-room + kitchen unit at some point? Or a living unit that includes a parents' apartment? At a minimum, this requires well-positioned sanitary facilities.

For purchasers and real estate developers, the trend toward small apartments is as understandable as it is profitable: demand remains high, they are readily placed on the market, require only a manageable financial investment, and are readily sold if the need should arise. This successful model thrives on singles, commuters, and young professionals. Micro-apartments, including the classical student apartment, are ideal investment properties.

Everything is listening to us: control via voice command

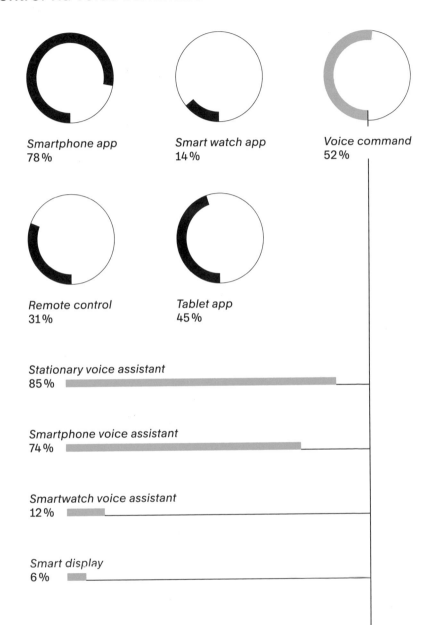

Smartphone app
78%

Smart watch app
14%

Voice command
52%

Remote control
31%

Tablet app
45%

Stationary voice assistant
85%

Smartphone voice assistant
74%

Smartwatch voice assistant
12%

Smart display
6%

The Apartment Search

BERLIN

PARIS

amsterdam

TOKYO

Reduction:
Why Is Easy Living So Hard?

Dublin

STOCK HOLM

"Light living" is a label for the ideal of our time, promoted by digital dematerialization and the explicit admonition, delivered by a variety of various advisors, to simplify your life. And of course, we already own everything – often, we simply have too much. The accumulation of things emerged relatively late in the history of humankind.[33] Visiting an old farmhouse, we often find little more than a niche in the hallway that serves as storage for the most important possessions: no shelves, no storage area. The hole in the wall suffices for keys and kerosene lamps. For articles of clothing, there were simply hooks on the wall (the wealthy could afford chests). A century ago, an ordinary household contained perhaps 200 objects. Today, it is 20 times that – 10,000 or so. At the same time, many objects have been deprived of their earlier significance. Sunday tableware was proudly displayed in sideboards, signifying culture, but in particular the host's social status. Then there were shelf units, with spaces reserved for this or that. Today, a plasma screen, having half the width of the wall, suffices. This has the advantage that the last remaining books can be piled up and digitalized. Things have become self-evident. You simply have them. Or no longer, perhaps (at least not visibly). But no matter how much we share and declutter, we can hardly exist without order. Visible chaos, however, often generates its antithesis: positively Spartan residential landscapes. The more messy types[34] and preppers there are (with their pallets of hoarded corned beef, beans, and rice, not to mention batteries, radios, protective vests, and tools, all held in reserve for the Great Catastrophe), the more organized domestic ascetics and sticklers for order there are as well.

But let us return now to superabundance, a product not least of all of a highly differentiated society, and of a heavily equipped industry that devises the perfect attire for every sporting activity. Constantly at the ready is the right costume for the fitness studio, for cycling, for yoga, even for Pilates. We experience an explosion of equipment directly on our own bodies. Frank Trentmann, a professor of history at Birkbeck College at London University, refers to this phenomenon as the "Empire of Things." A researcher into everyday life and consumer behavior, he remarks that "[...] what is excessive and superfluous is relative. There is no fixed line between 'needs' and 'wants.'"[35] First comes food, then the Tiffany lamp,

035

to abbreviate the Maslowian "hierarchy of needs," published by the psychologist in 1943. "If one need is satisfied, then another emerges,"[36] propounded Abraham Maslow. Is this, then, the reason we pile up objects intended to simplify life, which then begin to drown entire apartments like quicksand? At which point, gaining control over this flood becomes a genuine challenge.

Providentially, there is self-storage, supplemental space located at the edge of town, and an illustration of how readily we delegate problems. Out of sight, out of mind – just like climate change. Live and let accumulate: these days, we simply stockpile our stuff out of sight. Available external storage units range from one to one and 100 m², with units up to three meters in height. Professionals have a rule of thumb: in size, a storage unit must be between 10 and 15% of your apartment. It's as though all of the air between objects has been extracted, with crates stacked on chairs and sofas all the way up to the ceiling. An apartment measuring 100 m² is condensed down into a storage unit that measures between 10 and 15 m². Is it worth it? In the countryside, perhaps not, but in cities, where apartments with pantries and large basements are in short supply, many people, according to expert Christian Lohmann, resort to an external storage as an "extended living space."[37] Self-storage units are located along traffic arteries and arranged in such a way that you can simply call, come by with a vehicle, sign a contract, and deposit items into storage the very same day. With an access code and a chip card, the unit is accessible 24/7. Startups even offer a round-the-clock service that picks up your boxes from the front door. As a reminder of all the objects that are removed now from your field of vision, providers offer apps that allow your belongings to be uploaded as photos. Conceivably, you could even use them to make a photo album – but where would you keep it?

Critics might object that this is just a clever business model for capitalizing on our tendency toward hoarding. That depends entirely upon your perspective. Whoever finds themselves moving house to avoid storing ski equipment in the wardrobe will gratefully embrace self-storage as a smart alternative; those who find themselves accumulating more and more objects are only displacing the problem. But don't worry. We're in good company. Evidently, Picasso too was a passionate collector (hoarder?). When one apartment began to overflow, he would simply shut it up and move on to the next one. Admittedly, that sounds like a luxury solution.

So what does all of this collecting, saving, and space-saving storage tell us about our society? Mainly that we find ourselves in a state of upheaval. We lay claim to more resources, space, and energy than any generation before us – and we've begun to bump into the limits of the possible. Living space no longer keeps pace. When we consider metropolises like Tokyo, London, Zürich, and Munich, it seems plausible to say that self-storage is not just an expression of abundance, but also unavoidable if we are to tuck away our belongings in as little space as possible. Meanwhile, societal codes have changed. What strikes us as excessive may be an expression of wealth and social status in other cultures. In India, status is displayed on the wrist, in the form of gold chains. Instead, we have cell phones with exotic vacation photos, functional clothing, and even, at times, automobiles.

In a state of emergence for some time now is a tendency that runs counter to immoderate consumerism: the idea is to have less, but with greater awareness. Sharing rather than purchasing. Purging as an approach to rediscovering ourselves, along with our own suppressed needs. Or so runs the argument. The notion was already promoted by Socrates. "I hold that to need nothing is divine, and the less a man needs the nearer does he approach divinity." Today, 2400 years later,

Werner Tiki Küstenmacher and Lothar J. Seiwert created a bestseller out of the idea: "simplify your life – live more simply and more happily,"[38] launching a miniature simplification industry consisting of books, calendars, and counseling. The disconcerting aspect? Inherent even in the simple is a drive toward expansion, and – it must be confessed, regrettably – toward complexity.

It is not yet particularly clear where the "empire of things" actually leads. Concepts like the "clean desk policy" ensure a kind of brutal office orderliness. Whoever shares a desk, or no longer even has one at all, must ensure that each evening, all of the notepads, writing implements, and memos have been cleared away and an orderly work surface is surrendered to a successor. The model "simplify your work" is valid for life more generally. We simply cannot avoid the process of decluttering, purging, relinquishing, sharing. And when nothing else works, there are still solutions for disposing of our growing excess: drawstring trash bags, glass recycling containers, trash cans.

The Apartment Search

Cohabitation:
Changing Lifestyles –
Changing Cities

The Hybrid Home

At the urban level as well, life and work are tending to converge with one another. The combination of residential and office buildings is no longer an exotic species – nor are shopping districts that offer a mixture of hotels, gastronomy, and fitness 24/7. Found clustered around green courtyards on roofs today are residences you would otherwise expect to encounter on the urban periphery. The separation between commercial zones, office wastelands, and bedroom communities – promoted by the automobile – is hardly an eternal verity. And what about the return of tradespeople to the city? Undoubtedly, the new community calls for compromise, and perhaps even a renunciation of certain privileges and habits. A densified city requires tolerance, a new balance between life and work, between generations, cultures, and model of life.

In recent years, society has become increasingly diverse, variegated, differentiated. Conceptions of housing have changed as well, investing it with the potential to become more versatile and motley. And this is coming to pass, although some floor plans evidently conspire to perpetuate standards, now cast in stone, from a bygone era. Small wonder, then, that one of the most important exhibitions of recent years was designed to shed light on the "New Architecture of the Collective."[39] Curators Ilka and Andreas Ruby regard the normative housing culture of the 20th century, with its orientation toward the bigenerational family structure, as an anomaly: "For centuries, people tended to live and work in multigenerational households. For economic and social reasons as well, it seemed practical for people to form collectives in order to care for one another."[40]

Residential communities and cooperatives are on the upswing, along with new mixed forms: coliving, coworking, couch surfing, and "temporary living." In the wake of living experiments such as communes and residential communities, they see the future instead in cluster layouts, a group ensemble of apartments, each with its own kitchenette and bathroom. Common rooms alternate with private areas. Elective community, then – as the counterpole to cocooning, the more or less voluntary withdrawal into one's own four walls. But much speaks against such encapsulation. Housing specialist Mathias Müller, who is the managing director of EM2N Architekten AG Zürich/Berlin, believes that public space is on the rise: "People want to meet, to exchange ideas." He regards cocooning as a compulsive act, while the megatrend toward smaller and smaller households continues without interruption.[41] The larger question remains: in times of scarce living space, what is the general direction of development for the contemporary apartment? Where are the new forms of collective life, where are the genuinely experimental, even avantgarde housing projects?[42] Müller remained skeptical: through cheap capital, paradoxically, housing construction since the financial crisis has increasingly become one of the few investment opportunities that still promises a decent return. "Massive price increases (land and building costs) and shortages are a result of this excess demand." Unfortunately, he says, this means "poor framework conditions for unconventional, experimental, or collective housing projects."[43]

The polar opposite of the experimental is the freestanding single-family home with pitched roof and surrounding greenery – the successful model of the years of the "economic miracle," when no one gave a thought to climate change or CO_2 pricing. On the contrary. Growth was vital, intrinsically desirable. Even workers had the right to realize their dreams of a private home. And all of this was politically desirable. "Housing policy is the foundation of family policy,"[44] declared Konrad Adenauer in 1964. The idea was that landed property promotes stability: whoever has something to lose is oriented toward the present, and is immune to the temptation of a chancy world revolution. What didn't the German government do to promote the dream of property ownership? There was the housing subsidy introduced in 1952, a home ownership subsidy that elapsed in 2006, all the way to a controversial subsidy for home purchasers with children. But none of these benefits could obscure the fact that at times, the self-evident no longer appeared quite so obvious. For many, the dream of homeownership has collapsed – and from an environmental perspective, it may be a good thing too. The number of building permits for single-family homes has dropped by half over the past 20 years, with permits for multifamily dwellings rising by approximately 50%.[45]

Despite numerous new buildings, the housing question remains unresolved. Among the numerous voices on the topic, we might single out Christopher Dell's analysis of "housing as a commodity,"[46] which links the housing question to political economy, exposing the "commodification of urban space." If architecture is "frozen music" (to paraphrase Schopenhauer), then many shopping streets instead resemble three-dimensional Excel spreadsheets. Is the same true of housing? Recently, a cap on rent increases in the Federal State of Berlin met with failure.[47] Germany and Switzerland are classical renter countries,[48] with ownership lying below 50%,[49] far lower than European norms. It has become commonplace to say that each renter pays for his apartment in the course of his lifetime – or hers, or instead the landlord's. In its advertisements, the Mainz Savings Bank[50] claims unabashedly that homeownership brings happiness. A study[51] conducted by the University of Hohenheim on commission from the LBS Stiftung Bauen und Wohnen appears to confirm this: even controlling for factors like income, education level, and age, property owners are happier than renters. One's "own four walls," evidently, are something more than bricks and mortar: they are built psychology, and promise status and a sense of security. On the other hand, argues the Swiss architect Ernst Hubeli in his polemic "The New Crisis of the Cities,"[52] housing always means social policy. In recent decades, Hubeli argues, land use has led to "a social and economic crisis in our cities." For urban planners, the housing question is actually a question of land. We must, he argues, siphon off increasing land prices for the benefit of society as a whole, which has, in the end, covered all of the investments that allow land prices to rise in the first place: streets and childcare centers, universities and theaters, subway systems and other public amenities. Such considerations are nothing new. A glance at Article 161, Paragraph. 2 of the Bavarian Constitution reveals a highly topical passage: "Any increase of the value of the land which arises without special effort or capital expenditure of the owner shall be utilized for the general public."[53] Former SPD chairman Hans-Jochen Vogel mentions this passage in his book *Mehr Gerechtigkeit!* (More Fairness!)[54] – it is said to be his legacy.

Housing is not an absolute. Instead, it is a system of communicating tubes, into which norms and laws flow, along with funding options and interest rates, not to mention images of the "good life" and of a future in which human beings want to live. The apartment absorbs wider societal developments and endows them with visible form. Often, the way we live is only conditionally related to the way we want to live. When it comes to housing, desire and reality have rarely been so far apart as in today's rental market, which clearly favors owners. The market offers two options, but ultimately, one must be able to afford them. Which is fine when it comes to a tolerable compromise that balances location, condition, and equipment. Moreover, neighborhoods change, but this need not necessarily mean gentrification. It's enough for low income earners to yield to price pressure, ceding space to high earners. However, this hardly opens up adequate space for housing experimentation.

The home office[55] has the effect of a liberation vis-à-vis the functionally segregated city of modernity, neatly divided into areas for industry, commerce, and residence according to the principles of the Congrès Internationaux d'Architecture Moderne (CIAM) of Athens – an ill-advised development, together with the ideology of the car-friendly city. This means that the home office has also been caught up in a very different conflict – one that pits ecology and community against turbocapitalism and the unrestrained exploitation of resources. And although no one can precisely define the ecobalance of this labor model, it is clear that it eliminates many trips to the workplace, together with business trips that involve considerable stress – often with few concrete gains. It's worth reminding ourselves just how pleasant video chats have been in the age of COVID, with the participants allowing one another to speak, genuinely listening, and searching for real solutions. In this sense, the home office is a leap into premodern times in conjunction with the most up-to-date communication technologies – and simultaneously a component of an ecological shift.

Our lives continue to be shaped by the paradoxical, the indecisive, the simultaneous. Will the digital city, with its various platforms of the sharing economy, ultimately prove beneficial? At this point, it is hard to predict whether idealists will set the agenda, or instead investors, who will exploit the new collective consciousness (which emerges, often, from pure necessity) to create the ultimate moneymaking machine.

The Apartment Search

How many people live in a household?

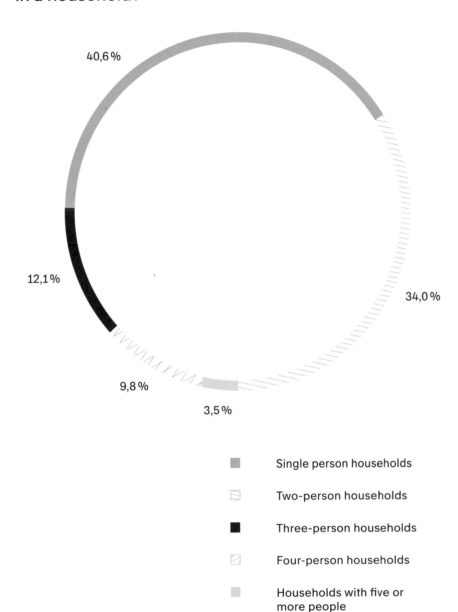

40,6 %

12,1 %

9,8 %

3,5 %

34,0 %

■ Single person households

▤ Two-person households

■ Three-person households

▨ Four-person households

▨ Households with five or
more people

The Apartment Search

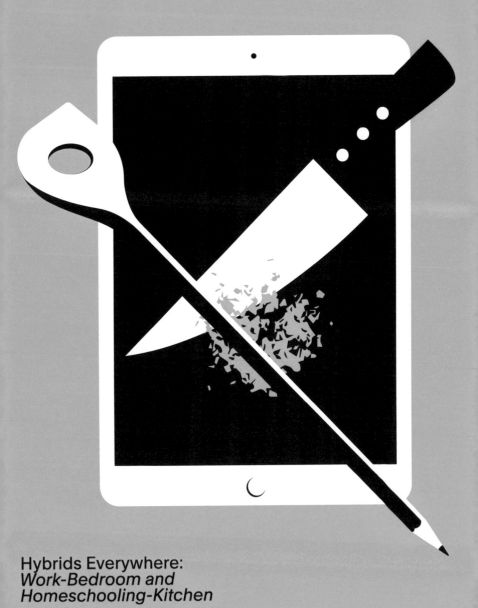

Hybrids Everywhere:
Work-Bedroom and
Homeschooling-Kitchen

The dissolution of self-contained apartments commenced long ago. It begins with functions – rooms are supplanted by zones, atmospheres predominate – and extends to new approaches for organizing cohabitation. In 2016, when the Cologne Furniture Fair asked Sebastian Herkner to design the House of the Future, he created a transparent, circular structure devoid of genuinely separate spaces, aside from bathroom and bedroom, and consisting of barrier-free zones separated by curtains. Herkner played with varying degrees of transparency. At the center, an open courtyard, plus a table where everyone eats together. What a picture!

How far does such hybridization extend? Work-bedrooms and homeschooling-kitchens are not the only crossbreeds of our time. In essence, modern life itself has become a hybrid, a condition that exists in a kind of in-between, a not-yet. It was the Swiss journalist and author Tom Kummer who astutely designated this condition as the "in-between." It is our fate to exist between continents, cultures, obligations, and time zones. The New Sisyphus must deal with many things simultaneously, and with zero downtime: pending calls, Tweets and Retweets, status reports and e-mails, along with daily decisions, family, and partnerships.

With its usurpation of ever new areas, the accelerated society penetrates deeply into our lives. The "new work," the permanent home office, and the 24-hour office make it impossible to just switch off. We compensate through evasive maneuvers, by hacking the system. In mid-2019, a tragicomic story circulated: more and more Japanese were leasing rental cars, but never moving from the spot. They simply worked there, or took a nap. This place of retreat is popular in particular because it costs very little, since prices for using rental vehicles are mainly calculated by the kilometer.[56] Not exactly cozy, at least according to European standards. Nowadays, of course, we use the term "hygge":[57] "cozy" sounds too petit-bourgeois.

The automobile as a place of retreat – there's probably something to it. In Europe as well, the private vehicle repre-

The Apartment Search

sents the last morsel of freedom for millions of commuters, accompanied by droning music or a good audio book: an undefined time oasis embedded in the daily grind. In every traffic jam, the automobile is transformed into a rolling office, with mobile Internet and soft upholstery. What would autonomous vehicles have to offer? The navigating work or recreation space is, definitively, no longer an automobile. Emerging here is something radically new, something that as yet lacks a real name. Our era is defined by the undefined; mirrored in the in-between, in our hybrid life and work routines, is a dynamic society that has jettisoned all stable rules.

The same is true for home sweet home, for the apartment. Its actual use is always far ahead of the floor plan. And even if we are forced to adapt to the residential boxes of the past, we continually explode their limitations. We undermine the determinism of pre-placed light switches and ceiling outlets. We improvise and investigate new spaces of freedom. Rooms with fixed functions are so yesterday. The in-between dominates, zones that cannot be fully defined, since digitalization means that freedom and control increase concurrently, necessitating a new balance. While we explode categories, however, we also need new words for the work-bedroom and the homeschooling-kitchen, zones for hanging out, gaming spots. Nothing is what it used to be, but we'll figure things out as we go along.

1   Kurt Tucholsky, "Das Ideal", 1927. See mumag.de/gedichte/tuc_k02.html.

2   See Peter Faller, *Der Wohngrundriss. Untersuchung im Auftrag der Wüstenrot Stiftung,* Munich 2002, esp. pp. 59–80.

3   See boeckler.de/de/boeckler-impuls-unbezahlbare-mieten-4100.html; faz.net/-gz7-acq63

4   Sonja Fröhlich, "Warum Erwachsene lieber in eine WG ziehen", *Hannoversche Allgemeine Zeitung,* 3 April 2016. haz.de/Sonntag/Top-Thema/Zusammen-ist-man-weniger-allein-Wohntrend-Erwachsenen-WG. See also Henrik Rampe, "WG für Berufstätige: Mehr als ein Zweckbündnis. Nicht nur Studis, auch immer mehr Menschen jenseits der dreißig ziehen in WGs. Was treibt Professorinnen und Familienväter dazu, sich mit anderen Kühlschrank und Putzdienst zu teilen?" *Frankfurter Allgemeine Zeitung,* 9 June 2021. faz.net/-gz7-acaxf.

5   Letter from Ludwig Mies van der Rohe, 27 May 1926, MoMA, Mies van der Rohe Archive, New York. Cited from Vittori Magnago Lampugnani, *Die Stadt im 20. Jahrhundert. Visionen, Entwürfe, Gebautes,* Berlin, 2010, vol. 1, p. 341.

6   See also Oliver Herwig, "Die Weißenhofsiedlung in Stuttgart," architare.de/de/magazin/die-weissenhof siedlung-stuttgart

7   See Hartmut Häußermann, Walter Siebel, *Soziologie des Wohnens. Eine Einführung in Wandel und Ausdifferenzierung des Wohnens,* Munich, 1996, p. 19; Jürgen Hasse, "Was bedeutet es, zu wohnen?" *Bundeszentrale für Politische Bildung,* 15 June 2018. bpb.de/apuz/270878/was-bedeutet-es-zu-wohnen-essay

8   See Stefan Kofner, "Übers Wohnen", hogareal.de/html/ubers_wohnen.html.

9   Boris Holzer, "Die Logik des guten Geschmacks. Intellektuelle schauen Serien und hören Rap. Aber elitär muss es sein," *Frankfurter Allgemeine Sonntagszeitung,* 1 August 2021. Including a reference to the study by Clayton Childress, Shyon Baumann, Craig Rawlings, Jean-Francois Nault, "Genres, Objects, and the Contemporary Expression of Higher Status Tastes", Sociological Science 8 (2021), pp. 230–264. DOI: 10.15195/v8.a12.

10 "Weibliche Selbstinszenierung in den neuen Medien. Ergebnisse einer Studienreihe, präsentiert von der MaLisa Stiftung, Januar 2019," malisastiftung.org/wp-content/uploads/ Selbstinszenierung-in-den-neuen-Medien.pdf. See also: verbraucherbildung.de/meldung/die-macht-der-bilder-selbstinszenierung-jugendlicher-im-internet.

11 InStyle, (2018), *Wer seine Wohnung früh weihnachtlich dekoriert, ist glücklicher,* instyle.de/lifestyle/weihnachten-frueh-dekorieren

12 Statistic from 1 November 2020: ard-zdf-online studie.de/files/2020/0920_Beisch_Schaefer.pdf.

13 See malisastiftung.org/wp-content/uploads/ Selbstinszenierung-in-den-neuen-Medien.pdf, p. 9.

14 ntv, 13 December 2013, "Album ohne Vorankündigung Beyoncé landet Coup," n-tv.de/11914661.

15 From the Latin *privatus:* "isolated, separate"; definition from: de.wikipedia.org/wiki/Privat

16 Article 13 of the Basic Law of the Federal Republic of Germany. de.wikipedia.org/wiki/Artikel_13_des_Grund gesetzes_f%C3%BCr_die_Bundesrepublik_ Deutschland.

17 See Terence Riley, *The Un-Private House: Museum of Modern Art,* New York City, 1999. p. 9. See also: moma.org/calendar/exhibitions/ 192.

18 See Oliver Herwig, "Hotelification oder das leichte Leben," *Lifeathome,* 13 November 2018. lifeathome.ch/2018/11/hotelification-oder-das-leichte-leben-oliver-herwig/.

19 See Kersten Augustin, Julia Friedrichs, "Wird erledigt," *Die Zeit,* 3 November 2016. zeit.de/2016/46/online-plattformen-angestellte-lieferdienste-dienstboten; work-watch.de/2017/07/die-revolte-der-neuen-dienstboten; Georgia Palmer, "Die Revolte der neuen Dienstboten," *taz,* 22 July 2017. taz.de/Arbeitsbedingungen-bei-Foodora-und-Co/!5428832/.

20 See Lena Graefe, "Statistiken zum Reiseverhalten der Deutschen," *Statista,* 12 July 21. de.statista.com/themen/1342/reiseverhalten-der-deutschen/

21 B. Joseph Pine II, James H. Gilmore, *The Experience Economy: Work Is Theater & Every Business a Stage,* Boston, Harvard Business School Press, 1999. conversationagent.com/2016/05/13/index.html

22 Swiss Office of Statistics bfs.admin.ch/bfs/de/home/statistiken/ tourismus/reiseverhalten.html.

The Apartment Search

23 See globenewswire.com/en/news-release/ 2014/01/30/924112/0/en/New-Report-on-Luxury-Buying-Spotlights-Cities-and-Customer-Segments.html; bcg.com/publications/2014/consumer-products-dealing-with-new-complexity-business-luxury.

24 tophotel.de/auswirkungen-der-krise-und-zukunftsprognosemarktreport-serviced-apartments-2021-veroeffentlicht-97262.

25 Lena Graefe, "Für welche Zwecke nutzt Ihr Unternehmen Serviced Apartments?" de.statista.com/statistik/daten/studie/992303/ umfrage/umfrage-unter-unternehmen-welt weit-zur-nutzung-von-serviced-apartments/.

26 justimmo-websites.s3.eu-central-1.amazonaws. com/551d18b8cb24ed0cccea76b03d73cef-de05cd76a/source.

27 Survey of experts by Oliver Herwig from 2015. See also destatis.de/DE/Presse/Pressemit teilungen/2020/07/PD20_269_122.html; destatis.de/DE/Presse/Pressemitteilungen/ 2020/11/PD20_N073_122.html.

28 Brit Glocke, *"Wir werden sehr viel flexibler leben."* ahgz.de/hoteldesign/news/wir-werden-sehr-viel-flexibler-leben-264126.

29 See bib.bund.de/DE/Service/Presse/2013/ 2013-07-Pro-Kopf-Wohnflaeche-erreicht-mit-45-m2-neuen-Hoechstwert.html.

30 Of course, this is only an average. See destatis.de/DE/Presse/Pressemitteilungen /2020/07/PD20_281_31231.html.

31 *Bundesbaublatt*, 5/2014, *"Klein, kleiner, mikro"* bundesbaublatt.de/artikel/bbb_Klein_kleiner_ mikro_1987397.html.

32 Oliver Herwig, interview with Dietrich Fink: "the question is not whether we want to intensify. In growth reasons, densification occurs daily. The question is whether we want to plan den-sification processes, for the sake of the spatial future of inhabitants, the beauty of the city, and the participation in profit from building rights ((Baurechtsgewinnen)) for urban society."

33 See also Oliver Herwig, "Sucht und Ordnung," *Lifeathome*, 18 September 2018. lifeathome.ch/2018/09/sucht-und-ordnung/.

34 Werner Gross, "Messie-Syndrom: Löcher in der Seele stopfen," *PP 1*, edition of September 2002, p.419. aerzteblatt.de/archiv/33777/Mes-sie-Syndrom-Loecher-in-der-Seele-stopfen

35 Frank Trentmann, *The Empire of Things: How We Became a World of Consumers from the 15th Century to the 21st*, New York, 2016. p.407.

36 de.wikipedia.org/wiki/Maslowsche_ Bed%C3%BCrfnishierarchie.

37 See rp-online.de/nrw/panorama/self-storage-bei-lagerbox-in-duesseldorf-ein-leben-in-der-blechbox_aid-17612239; sueddeutsche.de/geld/die-miet-box-kommt-verlaengertes-wohnzimmer-1.593188.

38 Werner Küstenmacher, Lothar J. Seiwert, *Simplify your Life. Einfacher und glücklicher leben*, Frankfurt am Main, 2004.

39 *Together! The New Architecture of the Collective*, ed. Mateo Kries, Mathias Müller, Daniel Niggli, Andreas Ruby, Ilka Ruby, Vitra Design Museum, Weil am Rhein, 2017.

40 Oliver Herwig, *"Together!"* kap-forum.de/together/.

41 Oliver Herwig, "Zusammenhalten. Die neue Architektur der Gemeinschaft. Interview," kap-forum.de/zusammenhalten/.

42 See Niklas Maak, "Häuser für eine andere Welt," *Frankfurter Allgemeine Zeitung*, 21 June 2021. faz.net/-gsa-ac73m.

43 Oliver Herwig, "Zusammenhalten. Die neue Architektur der Gemeinschaft. Interview," kap-forum.de/zusammenhalten/.

44 Hans Dietmar Schneider, Elisabeth Hoffmann, *Familienförderung durch Wohneigentum. Kindern ein Zuhause geben*, Konrad-Adenauer-Stiftung e. V., Sankt Augustin/Berlin, 2018. kas.de/documents/252038/3346186/Familien foerderung+durch+Wohneigentum.pdf/ 97a2388c-7b79-1968-08fd-4e05803b3ec4?

45 See Mark Fehr, "Fünf ernüchternde Fakten zum Mieten, Kaufen und Wohnen," *Frankfurter Allgemeine Zeitung*, 17 May 2021. faz.net/-hx6-abgx5.

46 Christopher Dell, *Ware: Wohnen. Politik. Ökonomie. Städtebau*, Berlin, 2013.

47 mietendeckel.berlin.de/. See also Oliver Herwig, "Ware Wohnen oder das wahre Wohnen: Wem gehört die Stadt?" *Frankfurter Rundschau*, 19 August 2020. fr.de/kultur/gesellschaft/wem-gehoert-die-stadt-90025881.html.

48 See Statista Research Department, "Wohneigen-tumsquote in ausgewählten Ländern Europas 2019," *Statista*, 15 December 2020. de.statista.com/statistik/daten/studie/155734/ umfrage/wohneigentumsquoten-in-europa/.

49 See destatis.de/DE/Themen/Gesellschaft-Umwelt/Einkommen-Konsum-Lebens

bedingungen/Vermoegen-Schulden/Tabellen/
haus-grundbbesitz-evs.html.

50 Daniel Hörner, "So wohnen wir", *Sparkasse Mainz*, 26 November 2019:
meine.sparkasse-mainz.de/immobilien/
so-wohnen-wir-die-wohneigentumsquote-
in-deutschland/.

51 Dorothea Elsner, "Macht Wohneigentum glücklich?", Study conducted by Hohenheim University, 5 May 2015.
komm.uni-hohenheim.de/112943?tx_ttnews%
5Btt_news%5D=27588&cHash=
ba2bb31e5341dc80d157d1bf653cdebf;
komm.uni-hohenheim.de/uploads/media/
Wohnglueck_broschuere.pdf.

52 Ernst Hubeli, *Die neue Krise der Städte. Zur Wohnungsfrage im 21. Jahrhundert*, Zürich, 2020.

53 bayern.landtag.de/fileadmin/Internet_
Dokumente/Sonstiges_P/BV_Verfassung_
Englisch_formatiert_14-12-16.pdf.

54 Hans-Jochen Vogel, *Mehr Gerechtigkeit! Wir brauchen eine neue Bodenordnung – nur dann wird auch Wohnen wieder bezahlbar*, Freiburg im Breisgau, 2019.

55 See also Oliver Herwig, "Die Welt nach Corona. Wer schützt das Home vor dem Office?", *Frankfurter Rundschau*, 9 June 2020.
fr.de/politik/raum-zeit-dilemma-13793254.html.

56 See Oliver Herwig, "Lob des Zwischenraums. Essay. Transformational Buildings, 2021,"
transformational-buildings.de/lob-des-
zwischenraums;
Christoph Neidhart, "Warum Japaner Autos mieten – und nirgends damit hinfahren", *Süddeutsche Zeitung*, 10 July 2019.
sueddeutsche.de/panorama/japan-auto-
mieten-schlafen-1.4518078.

57 "Hygge, happiness, and much more!", at *Visit Denmark*, visitdenmark.com/denmark/
things-do/hygge.

Why avoid setting up a smart home?

Personal

Smart home devices are too expensive for me
42%

Their use is too complicated
41%

Installation is too complex for me
33%

I find the benefit to be too minimal
31%

I experience a smart home as somehow ominous
6%

Security

I'm afraid of hacker attacks
34%

Fear of having personal data misused
33%

Privacy concerns
24%

Technical

The solutions aren't yet fully developed technically
20%

I'm unable to repair/maintain the devices independently
12%

Lack of compatibility
10%

The Apartment Search

Rooms and Dreams:
Apartment Viewing

Apartment Viewing

The nicest room:
nothing more than a bed,
a table at the window,
a wardrobe.

Tomas Espedal,
Biografie, Tagebuch, Briefe,
Berlin, 2017

What is it that makes the experience of dwelling so enthralling in the 2020s? Essentially, it is the way in which opposites converge within a confined space, demanding solutions. Home life is wedged uncomfortably between contemporary requirements and standardized floor plans. Exploding real estate prices are causing our dreams of spacious flats in prewar buildings with gardens to simply collapse. At the same time, the Internet opens up possibilities for overcoming spatial restrictions on location, at least technically (and conceptually).

Observable here is genuine momentum, and moreover in all rooms, which now take on multiple identities, transformed now into zones where all kinds of things take place simultaneously: the bathroom is upgraded into a wellness temple; the middle-class living room becomes an online couch; the fitted kitchen is exchanged for a living kitchen. Everything appears tidy and chic, perfect for posting. In the age of Instagram, even the bedroom mutates into a semipublic space. Some genuinely succeed in breaking through the four walls, not unlike the 'v' effect familiar from the theater which dissolves the fourth wall, so that spectators and players become one. The home becomes an online stage for daily life. Appropriately, one digital provider is called the "Nest": cocooning and digital access are not antagonistic, but instead condition one another reciprocally. And if Walter Benjamin referred to the nineteenth century as "addicted to dwelling," referring to the "residence as the receptacle for the person," which fitted him like a set of instruments residing in a compass case, which lie in "deep, usually violet, folds of velvet,"[1] then the new codependency is digital in nature. The immaterial web and its social networks enclose us just like the real residential casings of the nineteenth century. But even more snugly.

Our homes are characterized by reduction and hybridization. This also has an impact on furnishings: the writing table is little more than a stand for a tablet or notebook. Books disappear – and CD shelves are dismantled. Only the plasma screen defends its place in the family shrine. Everything else is in flux, flexibly at the service of temporary, multipurpose work-leisure-multimedia spaces. With the invasion of the office in the form of the home office, the final levee has been breached. The work/couch-bed and the file cabinet/dresser illustrate the constraints of daily optimization. Escalating at the same time are demands for storage space at the edge of town. For the standard floor plan of the optimized urban dwelling can accommodate (or finance) neither pantry nor wardrobe, to say nothing of a guest room or utility room – the very term already has an archaic ring. And with that, off we go to the apartment viewing.

Apartment Viewing

Prop Warehouse:
The Corridor

A magical moment, courtesy of Woody Allen: the door of an apartment swings open, the hostess smiles, the guest suddenly finds himself standing in the middle of the living room, surrounded by books, pictures, and pleasant conversation. Typically New York, one supposes, and recalling a personal invitation when the guests were crowded into the narrow corridor, suddenly so small and cramped. Entrances and hallways are hardly the strength of modern residential development. They simply exist, like the bargain counter of a department store. Which is how they look as well: crowded and devoid of lines. Some entrances resemble an obstacle course en route to work, with slippery runners, overhanging containers, and treacherous cables. Home experts recommend space consolidation, ideally in the form of large, built-in cupboards, which put an end to the plague of little objects. But this solution is often symptomatic of the problem itself: there is simply no space, certainly not for built-in cupboards.[2]

The corridor is a peculiar species. Despite being indoors, its wet clothing, odiferous shoes, car keys, and gloves are a constant reminder of the world outside. Then there are the unavoidable accessories: cupboard, shoe container, key rack, hooks, mirror. Nothing really fits; there is always a centimeter too little here or there. Imelda Marcos, for one, was a stranger to this problem. Her estimated twelve hundred pairs of shoes filled entire rooms, and meanwhile fit nicely in a museum in Manila, if not in the entrance area of an average apartment. But with no walk-in dressing room in sight, where are the shoes to go? Where to put the jacket, the coat, the rain cape? Not to mention the bunch of keys and the cell phone? The hallway has long since become a buffer zone for everyday life, filled with the most varied props, depending upon the weather and time of day. To boot, it also serves as an electrical interface with the world outside. Set into the wall are shoes, boxes, and telephone connections; earlier, there was the gray box for the Deutsche Post, decorated with a telephone bench and chair, today a tangle of cables, WLAN router, and adaptors, which some people conceal shamefacedly, and others simply allow to billow forth from the wall. If anything unites the objects found in the corridor, it is their function of demarcating a boundary line that no longer really exists. Here the private world, there the public one. Families here, friends there. Cozy inside, industrious outside – once upon a time. Just as work life has come to approximate an entire lifetime, the entrance to the apartment has changed – from a scenarized threshold to the sterile flow heater of everyday life, where you stand, gulping down an espresso, checking the latest tweets, along with your hair in the mirror.

Traditionally, architects tended to emphasize such transitional zones. They endowed the entrance of the lady of the house with a certain grandeur, giving shape to room-height doors, decorative trimmings, providing even the longest corridor with enough volume to accommodate a cabinet, a hat shelf, one or two armchairs, along with a side table. The ceremonial dimension still survived then, in theaters, operas, luxury hotels. Lingering on today from such design abundance and spatial luxury is little more than the vestibule, two steps that at times resemble an act of sabotage against baby carriages and walkers, to say nothing of wheelchairs and skiers with leg casts.

Even in apartment flats, the door to the outside is now secured by motion sensors, video surveillance, and number codes, which must be committed to memory if one wants to avoid embarrassing phone calls to an external security center, or even more embarrassing security questions on your cell phone ("What is the name of your cat?" or "What street do your parents live on?"). At any rate, the electronic armament of the threshold is hardly meaningfully proportionate to the area lying immediately behind it. If first impressions really were indispensable, we would have to be highly attentive to this space. The opposite is the case. The corridor is no longer the calling card of the home and its possessor, and is instead a transitional zone that inflicts significant wear on furniture and wall paint, and it is not only families with small children that are well aware of this.

Why is this the case? Well, the modern apartment sets priorities that are oriented toward affordable dimensions. An apartment measuring $80\,m^2$ can hardly accommodate an eat-in kitchen, master bedroom, wellness bathroom, and large entrance area all at the same time. Hence, the corridor – despite being the actual backbone of the apartment – becomes a kind of maneuverable architectural mass that facilitates the planning of the more "important" rooms. The larger the living room, the smaller the corridor. The nerve cord of the home is linked to all of the other rooms as a kind of communicating tube. Here, the modern movement bears a portion of the guilt. As early as 1924, when Bruno Taut enthused about the "big cleanup," he did not mean the pairs of underwear that had slipped between the sofa cushions: "When everything in the apartment, absolutely everything that is not immediately necessary to living, in accordance with the most severe and ruthless selection process, is ejected, then a new kind of beauty emerges as a matter of course." With digitalization, we are actually moving in this direction: even the constituents of an intellectual household can meanwhile be accommodated on tablets or plasma screens, and what remains is a materials storage for everyday life.

Years ago already, the Munich architect Peter Haimerl used a computer simulation to send virtual dust whirling through a floor plan in order to identify dead corners, perfect places for built-in cupboards and other useful components that generally get in the way: wardrobes, shoe cabinets, shelving. Only one recourse remains: radicalization. Either really large, or omitted entirely. This is also the view of Philipp Reichelt, a partner of Grünecker Reichelt Architekton: "A corridor should be spacious, or else simply dropped from the planning. As a pure connecting passageway, it is highly questionable."

No matter how you slice it, the modern hallway offers little by way of space. Small wonder so many home consultants advise disguising a corridor's cramped dimensions optically through the use of (pale) colors. When the rolling container lands under the stairs again, and the new shoes do not fit into the shoe cabinet, a certain equanimity is called for. The neighbors also have to do this when the bobby car races around the shared hallway again on a rainy day. Unless it's simply too narrow to serve this purpose.

Apartment Viewing

The Beating Heart:
The Kitchen

Ettore Sottsass was notorious for sneaking into his host's kitchen during evening soirées. As a designer, he was fond of the "secret places behind the scenes, where the ingredients were prepared for a kind of sacred performance." And today, while certain recipes' secrets remain, this stage offers itself up willingly to spectators. We cook together, dining in a circle of friends that gathers around the kitchen island, just like the members of a clan gathering long ago around a campfire. The modern open-plan kitchen merges work and living, event and community.

Which has consequences for its organization. Entering a kitchen today, we often find ourselves standing amidst an open living area that is devoid of doors, service hatches, and even walls. Everyone sits together on the stage, hosts as well as guests. Tableware and cooking pots are presented ostentatiously, or else disappear like the upper cabinets of optimized small kitchens. Even gleaming steel surfaces, long the insignia of superior professionalism, are supplanted by wood and natural materials. At times, only a lonely water faucet betrays the fact that work actually goes on here. The equipment is there when in use, and is otherwise concealed behind eye-catching surfaces.

In Praise of the Living Kitchen

Nowhere is fashion as manifest as in the kitchen – along with the financial status of its users, needless to add. Trends race by in rapid succession. A fashion for the prestigious kitchen is succeeded by a mania for the space-optimized microkitchen. In European metropolises, some apartments are even dispensing with the stove: given exploding rental prices, a refrigerator and microwave will have to suffice. Whether (unavoidably) small or extravagantly large, all are united by a single ideal: the living kitchen has freed itself from the constraints of built-in solutions, and has again become a place of community. And everyone is raving about it. Immediately, we see a long table before us, where we can gather to enjoy cooking with friends. While one takes care of initial preparations, another uncorks the wine, under the pretext that it needs to breathe. Family and friends all come together here. Pots clatter, music and words resound through the space, there is an aroma of freshly chopped parsley, and for a brief moment, the clan has come together once again. Everyday life is forgotten. Every movement is right. We are together. We have a goal.

Actually, the living kitchen is a relic of the nineteenth century, something the modern movement strove to abolish: enough stale air and poor hygiene, enough of poorly proportioned apartment layouts. The optimized modernist kitchen was a little factory, modeled on rolling train kitchens. Every movement was calculated. In the space-saving galley kitchen, nothing was superfluous. In 1917, Hermann Muthesius spoke of "technical and hygienic spaces, such as bathrooms and kitchens, which breathe the spirit we know from the beautifully equipped machine rooms of large factories." His prognosis: "The interior decor of our apartments is becoming smooth, plain, and practical, having formerly been obtrusive and overloaded." The new culinary environment was exemplified by Margarete Schütte-Lihotzky's "Frankfurt Kitchen," its design conditioned by Taylorism. The Viennese architect sought to demonstrate that "simplicity and functionality not only conserve labor, but also, in association with good materials and good form and color," mean "clarity and beauty."[3] The result was the modern culinary laboratory with short distances and practical bins and compartments. Everything was carefully considered: food had its place – and so did kitchen scraps. Of course, Schütte-Lihotzky, although a great architect, never suspected that the functionally optimized kitchen would ultimately become the tiresome built-in kitchen, found in numberless micro-apartments, its name already redolent of frozen foods and ready-made meals.

The living kitchen 2.0 unites the best of both worlds: the communal open-plan kitchen and the technologically optimized Frankfurt Kitchen. What never quite worked in the shared flat should come off here. We no longer cook in seclusion while our guests crowd around the coffee table; now, they join in the fun. Here, there is nothing to hide – and the new cooking station looks the part: transformed into a living space, with parts of the kitchen frankly subdivided into a living-cooking room, all the more so when individual objects are no longer clearly assignable to the realm of steaming pots and savory odors, of cooking flames and food preparation, but are themselves display objects, like the series of gleaming copper pots that hang on the wall. The stage has been set. All that remains is a suitable occasion for inviting friends. The focus is on collective cooking, on the event character of the invitation. Everyone takes part, before sitting together at a long table, with cooking and dwelling nonchalantly mingling together.

A Question of Equipment:
The Status Kitchen

The freestanding kitchen block, with its virtually invisible cooker hood or integrated fume hood, is essentially standard in upscale homes. Along with elegant optics. Status is determined by the quality of the amenities – regardless of whether cooking actually takes place there or not. Materials take center stage, including those one would not expect to see around a stove, or were previously difficult to process: mixed spices are parked on magnetic surfaces, partition walls vanish at the touch of a button, high-performance ceramics promise scratch-proof surfaces, and Corian furnishings make gapless connections possible. Meanwhile, wood too is making a comeback in the cookscape: finely veined fruitwoods, combined with stone slabs for permanence.

On average, a built-in kitchen lasts for about 20 years,[4] depending on the original fittings and levels of daily use, and growing numbers of purchasers are opting for greater luxury when preparing food. For years now, the high-class kitchen has been in the ascendance. For everyone else, there is always the cell phone for a quick pizza delivery. When it comes to kitchens, opinions differ – not to mention budgets: wellness at the hearthside for LOHAS, speed cooking for everyone short on time or unprepared to spend it in the kitchen. Coexisting are the exclusive living kitchen and the space-optimized kitchen.

Filling side dishes are so yesterday: today, the wooden spoon is a part of science, if not art. We are conditioned to high performance in the kitchen, in the conviction that a simple if lovingly prepared meal no longer cuts it. There has to be a gimmick, a special seasoning, an unconventional combination, and of course the suitable wine. This has consequences: show me your equipment, and I'll tell you who you are. The steam cooker, shake mixer, and induction stove are only entry-level types, followed by the sous vide cooker, the wine refrigerator with various temperature zones, and the steam oven – and of course every ambitious hobby chef knows instantly what a planetary stirring system is.

In 2020, according to the German Federal Office of Statistics, an incredible 99.9% of households owned a refrigerator,[5] 86% owned a coffee maker, and 76.6% had a microwave. In some kitchens, you will find a singular pasta maker or a drying rack for homemade noodles, to be served with homegrown herbs and organic Wallonian butter. The overabundance of equipment in private households means that often, growth is possible only through replacement purchases. We already have everything, often double or in triplicate. All of the remnants of fluctuating culinary and kitchen fashions – wok, fondue pot, raclette grill, etc. – gather dust somewhere in a drawer.

A fate that may already threaten devices such as the Thermomix.

But where are all of these gadgets, updates, and upgrade kits to be stored? As early as the 1950s, experimental homes built by Walt Disney contained rotating, electrically operated wall units. Ever since, every kitchen has contended for storage space, partly because the pantry (which at times replaces a small refrigerator) has become a luxury – simply absent now from regular floor plans.

Stockpiling:
No Thanks!

COVID ushered in a change: supply inventories are no longer just for preppers and people who have survived hard times. Who knows where all of the extra toilet paper has been stashed: under the bed, between bookshelves, concealed under old homemade crocheted hats, or stacked neatly to form an archway above the toilet? Earlier, at any rate, there was a place where the stockpiling of supplies – which has enjoyed an astonishing revival of late – could be accommodated: in the pantry, together with dozens of Mason jars, canned goods, and jams. The "food store" (to use another antiquated term) was a mysterious place, cool and dry, and ideally, not far from the kitchen. It was the belly of the house, its culinary memory, simultaneously a miniature high-shelf warehouse and a land of milk and honey. But as in Paradise, a fall from grace was imminent.

There was always something tempting about a pantry, something unfathomable. The light source was a naked lightbulb that dangled high above your head, and there was something manic and military about the shelf organization. Heavy items were found below: bags of onions and potatoes, and above them, rows of cans: peas, beans, and oddities like corned beef. Above the tinned meat were homemade cherry preserves and other fruits. Finally, there was rice, eggs, and noodles, as well as vegetables from the kitchen garden. Originally, sausage hung from the ceiling, dried ham, game meat. There was no kiwifruit, no glass noodles, neither papaya nor zucchini. Even in the late 1970s, the pantry was filled with carbohydrates and non-perishables, which had to be regularly rotated and inspected: pans and preserves with the most recent expiration date in front, everything else was allowed to collect dust toward the rear. There would likely have been a supply of alcohol as well: beer and red wine, but the children weren't terribly interested in that. More tempting were the sweets, retreating somewhere into forgetfulness, and regarded at some point as "in the public domain." It somehow seemed right that the package of jelly beans lurking behind the jams should find their way to the bedroom to be enjoyed without parental supervision.

A pantry was practical, of course, but required a minimum of maintenance. This was covered by the weekly shopping list and the meal plan. Those who lost track might find themselves compelled to consume nearly-out-of-date provisions for seven days running. It would be such a shame to waste it. The pantry illustrated the ideal functioning of the organization known as the family – neat and tidy, and no surprises. Even for a family of three, there was quite an accumulation. A look at the statistics on "staple food supplies"[6] compiled by the Federal Ministry of Food and Agriculture for three people and twenty-eight days receives a remarkable overview: 29.4 kg of grains, bread, and potatoes. Along with 33.6 kg of vegetables and root vegetables, 21.6 kg of fruit, 168 liters of beverages, 22.2 kg of milk and dairy products, and finally, 12.6 kg of fish, meat, and eggs, as well as 3 kg of fats and oils. In times of panic buying, mother's disciplined shopping list no longer seems quite so silly. Suddenly, stockpiles are no longer adequate – a notion reminiscent of premodern times, when people cultivated their own gardens, and delivery services were unheard of. Incidentally, as early as 1926, in his lecture "The Modern Housing Estate," the architect and provocateur Adolf Loos recommended a degree of exaggeration: "The pantry can be overly large," he counseled. It serves as "storage for all fruits and vegetables."[7] Naturally, the Looshaus in the Werkbund Housing Estate in Vienna boasted a pantry alongside the kitchen on the ground floor. Hard times might always arrive.

At some point, meanwhile, the great hero of the pantry was over. Parallel to the just-in-time economy and overflowing supermarkets, it seemed almost insane to stockpile and maintain food supplies. Everything was available: all you had to do was reach out your hand to procure something for the evening meal, or simply have it delivered. Remaining in the basement was a kind of residual storehouse, and also darkened room with its surrender freezer, stuffed with meat of all kinds, pizza, vanilla ice cream, and French fries ready for frying.

Finally, the pantry seemed to be obsolete. But then preppers revealed that people were laying away supplies for X Day, the apocalypse, or the "revolution": a disquieting jumble of batteries, water purifiers, candles, canned goods, and conspiracy theories. Through COVID, we now know better – notwithstanding all of the services that deliver purchases in homeopathic doses just ten minutes after an order has been submitted. Panic buying can be rather monotonous.

A Little Psychology of the Kitchen

The place where a good party begins – and, as a rule, ends as well – is not a room, but instead a state of mind. An attitude toward life. It's where we live, check our mail, urge our kids to do homework, and engage in telelearning. Instinctively, the patchwork family gathers here. Trendsetters and creative workers are aggressive partisans of the kitchen, and many agree: the space around hearth and table is the paramount one. Which is why the living kitchen is the incarnation of a better world, a better community. A fondness for communal dining is not just reflected in the ratings of cooking shows, but in the sales figures of kitchen manufacturers as well.[8]

Certain everyday dramas, meanwhile, play themselves out between appetizers and the main course. The men showcase the latest technology – women have a flair for ambience. Beyond stereotypes, the oven seems to demarcate a dividing line between gender roles. While the wife shops in haste during the week alongside her day job, so to speak at a flat rate, her husband makes his purchases on holidays or on the weekend, a premium offer. Food preparation is a hobby that is taken seriously, and cooking paraphernalia serve as status symbols. Small wonder kitchen facilities have now become top priority, the ensemble – a mixture of high-tech (induction stove, meat thermometer, sous vide technology, precision scales) and basics (copper pots, gas stove) – overtaking even the family car in rank. Stressed-out managers are not alone in finding relaxation in their ovens, and without needing to lose control. The roast arrives à point or better: just in time on the table, ingredients weighed to the tenth of a gram, as specified by the cookbook, or instead improvised with panache. Such precision is encountered otherwise only among watch aficionados, and is mirrored increasingly in sophisticated kitchen planning which unites functionality with joie de vivre, leaving nothing to chance.

Evidently, the social ascendancy of the kitchen was unavoidable,[9] and is the flipside of thriving delivery services and convenience meals requiring little more than a brief visit to the microwave. The kitchen: here is the magic of a community that gathers here, despite existing in its classical form only with increasing rarity. Apparently, a parallel development is taking place. We are outsourcing more and more cooking competency to professionals, or picking up ready-to-eat meals that can be heated as quickly and easily as possible, only to pick up the cooking spoon again on weekends, hoping to reclaim some of what modern life has deprived us of through its efficiency: the joy of preparing a meal for oneself and others – even if this is performed with the assistance of a home chef meal kit, which not only takes over the trip to the market, but also provides successful recipes, to be followed step by step. Convenience is here as well. Cooking becomes quicker, and at the same time more sophisticated. How so? Expectations escalate – and with them the equipment used in our own cooking workshops. With COVID and the advent of the home office, many routines have changed: this was shown by a representative survey[10] according to which cooking took place in more than half of all German households in 2021. Or more precisely: in 52%; a COVID bonus of more than 10% over the previous year. Clearly, the kitchen is still in a state of change. Beckoning now is the Smart Kitchen,[11] with perpetually new online recipes (offering the culinary knowledge, so to speak, of the entire world). We will of course continue cooking in the future, but the resources we will use are changing rapidly.

App in the Kitchen!

What will the future bring? The induction stove, sous vide technology, and the meat thermometer arrived in upper-class households some time ago. The same is true of the steam oven. The next step is predictable enough: the kitchen will become interactive. Although it's premature to simply discard the wooden spoon, programmable baking ovens with integrated steam cookers are taking over much of the labor. Just enter the cooking time and the weight of the roast, and the program does the rest – to perfection. Full surface induction stoves know which pot sits where, and heat only these surfaces, with pinpoint accuracy.

Manufacturers have long since made it possible to network various devices with one another and the outside world. In a "smart home," the contents of your refrigerator can be called up from the supermarket on your tablet or smart phone. You buy exactly what you need – or the missing ingredient for a specific recipe. An optional "smart manager" even recommends recipes. Service, thanks to networked "white goods." By comparison, the trends currently promoted by the consortium "Die Moderne Küche" (The Modern Kitchen) seem rather outmoded: "Everything should proceed simply and intuitively, for example through voice or gesture control. Refrigerators and ovens respond to a word, a wave, or a fingertip. Appliances are networked with one another and with the domestic technology, the catchphrases being "connectivity" and "smart home." Assistive systems offer support with measurements and servicing, as well as with dishwashers or coffee machines. In open-plan homes, a priority is ensuring that all devices operate as quietly as possible. Functionality and energy-efficiency are held in a balance."[12]

The big kitchen battle turns on questions of calories and connectivity. And on the question of just how much information the ultimate kitchen aids of tomorrow will be able to gather autonomously about users. This is nothing new. Essentially, the kitchen is only now catching up with the telephone and automobile: assistive systems lend a hand – whether we want them to or not. Much occurs below the threshold of awareness. All that is required is users who actually appreciate it.

Apartment Viewing

Wellness Oasis:
The Bathroom

Earlier, which is to say before the real estate bubble took hold in German city centers, there were two killer criteria that gave renters or purchasers pause when considering a new home: there absolutely had to be a balcony – and the bathroom had to have a window. Regarding bathrooms at least, expectations have changed. The windowless bathroom with no outside wall has long become standard, a compromise without which most compact layouts would be difficult or impossible to implement. Of course, this has consequences for bathroom accoutrements. Not so much for runners or seat cushions (who still has these?), but instead for the lighting, to which users are exposed at the most sensitive times of day: morning and evening. No one, after all, wants to see a zombie staring back at them from the mirror. While earlier, halogen bulbs cast the flushed glow of morning on still drowsy bodies, today it is increasingly LED illumination that is capable of almost anything, even flooding the corner of the bathroom with the warm radiance of sunset, or conjuring special colors or luminous atmospheres for the night owls among bathroom visitors. Cold neon light or greenish power-saving bulbs are meanwhile a thing of the past, although they still exist in myriad forms, mainly in hotel chains, whose bathrooms are purchased as complete units and inserted into the shell construction like oversized capsules. Small wonder such fully plastic cubicles resemble nothing so much as substandard space debris.[13]

Overall, the form of temporary occupancy embodied to perfection by certain hotels has become the new benchmark of our own standards and needs. And such colors, materialities, and layouts are popping up more and more often among private developers. Suddenly, everything is as clean, perfect, and somehow sterile as on vacation, complete with beige walls, oiled wood, and multiple steam nozzles in the shower. Formerly, the imaginary home emanated from interior design magazines; today, we dream of living in a five-star hotel. With some very odd consequences. For example the bathtub (moist, warm) is found with greater frequency directly alongside the bedroom bed (which we like cool, but cozy under the covers). A decade or so ago, hotels began to merge the two intimate zones, making it possible to roll out of bed and right into the bathtub, although for the most part, the living space is separated from the shower and wash basin by glass partitions. Nice for a vacation, but is it practical long-term in one's own home? Behind all of this is a fundamental change in the quality of intimacy. Functions that were once bashfully concealed now compete with the perennially representative space of the living room. First it was the kitchen, where guests and hosts sit today together at a long table, then the bathroom, which has come to function as a little wellness temple, accommodating upscale demands. Water culture: the idea has seeped slowly from the aristocracy down to the middle-class working world.

In the Baroque era, it took pavilions crammed with Dutch tiles and water faucets with gilded dolphins' heads to introduce the Turkish bath into places where a distasteful odor often permeated the powdered and bewigged company. The first heated indoor pool since antiquity was installed in the Nymphenburg Palace Park between 1718 and 1722 by the principal court architect Joseph Effner. The bathhouse served the Bavarian Elector Max Emanuel as a place of erotic delight. But it took another century or so for Ludwig II to usher in such modernity in 1875. He had the famous Blue Grotto of Capri recreated in Linderhof Palace. Here, technology and romanticism became a dream couple that refuses to be parted even today. Wave machines and electrical lighting created a fantasy world: accompanied by strains of Wagner, the Swan King had himself rowed toward an artificial rainbow in a gilded shell boat. The consummate camp staging was made possible by an electrically operated projection apparatus. Today's wellness temple – despite its rain shower and sophisticated luminous atmospherics – seems modest by comparison.

But all of that is changing: cordless switches and networked systems are making new geometries possible. Ultraflat displays seem to disappear into the wall, or take the form of handy remote controls that allow easy manipulation of not just lighting and luminous colors, but water temperature, intensity, and the position of the shower stream as well. Soon, the smart bathroom may offer music wellness with hi-fi quality: the first manufacturers are offering acoustic bathtubs, components of an all-encompassing sound system consisting of structure-borne sound transducer and digital control box. Via Bluetooth, an entire music library is at your fingertips. Sound and water waves complement one another to perfection. Music promotes deep relaxation, and the bathtub becomes a resonating body.

In the future, bathroom manufacturers will offer even more: barrier-free bathrooms with "superior amenity quality." Modern technology roles regulate everything. There are precisely controllable massage showers, dimmable lights, aromas, and your favorite song upon awakening. In the bathroom of the future, the flick of a finger will suffice to regulate the lighting, a single word to adjust water temperature. Then there is bathroom geometry, which accommodates your postretirement as well.

No one ages overnight: it creeps up on you. At the least when it becomes a challenge to swing your leg over the edge of the bathtub, it might be time for a new bathroom, one that doesn't allow minor details to become daily impediments. Despite all of the barriers to accessibility still found in German homes, the bathroom could serve as an acceptable gateway for components that allow us to function in old age, while making life a bit easier for everyone in the meantime, an example being the level-access shower, which eliminates nasty trip hazards.

The bathroom has had an astonishing career as an everyday luxury commodity, from the simple cubicle to the super paddling pool, to a self-contained realm holistic experience that is tailor-made to our individual needs, with just the right temperature and soothing sounds. Soon, we will have achieved what the Romans dreamt of two thousand years ago. Water signifies not just hygiene and the body cult, but is also equated with wellness. And barrier-free floor plans, combined with cutting-edge technology, will hopefully allow us to remain in our own apartments well into old age.

Apartment Viewing

Hang-Out Lounge:
The Living Room

The analog living room is dead. Formerly a place of static furnishings and sparing use, it is now a multifunctional space where we eat, play, meet friends, and sometimes even watch television.[14]

For an astonishingly long time, the "parlor" resisted all of the upheavals of the modern age. Outside, the Cold War raged, the forests died out, and there were demonstrations against nuclear power and diesel engines: and all the while, the locus of bourgeois self-presentation continued to hibernate. Over time, the furniture may have grown paler, more lightweight, the wall units fragmenting into more or less transportable elements, but essentially, the living room remained a picture of good old analog times. And the glaring contradiction it embodied became increasingly manifest. Despite being rarely used, the living room occupied nearly one third of the total surface area of a typical apartment, between circa 20 and 50 m². And that is no longer sustainable.

Digital modernism has swept away many habits and accessories. Who sits at a table with a starched tablecloth and placemats while the children and guests chat, share, and link on mobile devices? Who still shows off their leaded crystal glassware to guests, when the motto today is 'simplify your life,' and white walls have become the quintessence of freedom and luxury? Who still purchases shelving by the meter when books and compact discs are sucked up by Spotify and digital reading devices? Who collapses into a heavy armchair, now that even the television, the long-serving successor to the home altar, is no longer the master of our leisure time, deposed now by the mobile device?

No matter how you look at it, the classical living room has surrendered its task as the showroom of culture, order, and affluence for the middle-class family. But what actually took place there? The Tübingen author Marcus Hammerschmitt recalls reluctantly: "The living room of my childhood and youth was an unyielding place, one that served representative

Apartment Viewing

functions. Characteristic of its rituals was formal meals on Sundays and holidays, simulated conviviality at family celebrations, the occasional television evening of the more apathetic variety." Hammerschmitt lists the constituent parts of the room: "The dining table stood there, the good tableware was stored there, it was after all the best room in the house. Only one thing was lacking: we never succeeded in inhabiting this room with the naturalness implied by its name." And how do things stand with the ingredients of homeyness, the furnishings? They are still present, albeit in altered form.

Monster Wall Unit in Oak

Of course, the wall unit still exists,[15] the three-piece upholstered set, the display case filled with souvenirs. But in fact, the good old living room is dead as a dormouse, just like all of those old monster cabinet walls in oak that dominated it. At one time, the cabinet stood for the inexorable ascendancy of the bourgeoisie, which ceaselessly collected objects and status symbols, and wanted finally to exhibit them, in imitation of the aristocratic and monastic cabinet walls of the sixteenth century. A Mannerist cabinet was both a piece of shrunken architecture, a tongue-in-cheek mixture of exuberant carving work (column, cornices, volutes), and a place to preserve documents and other items of importance. Monumental and immobile, it had an air of permanence. And it took some time for the cabinet to free itself of its decorative excess. In the nineteenth century, it was still representative and weighty.

The Bauhaus, particleboard, and geometry ushered in the turning point, and a new century the change in function. But the middle-class wall unit was not just more slender and delicate but also an oaken powerhouse. Well into the 1960s, it dominated a room that was far too small for it. Tables, chairs, and chests of drawers played second fiddle. It was the eye-catcher. Unbudgeable. As though crafted for eternity. Standing behind mechanically polished glass were goblets, while various cutlery trays lurked in drawers. Enthroned between book-club classics was the stereo hi-fi – the television hiding in shame in a cupboard, which paradoxically reinforced its prominence. Only when the cabinet doors were opened like the wings of an altar did the television make an appearance, an object of veneration around which the family would assemble, eager to receive the (often not particularly) glad tidings in the form of nightly newscasts. With the bashfully sacred stereo furniture, things came full circle. For the cabinet was always something more than a means for storing everyday objects. It was an idea, and harbored the promise of perpetual coziness. The cabinet had survived the chaos of war, remaining immutably itself. The world has changed, but the living room sideboard behaved as though the bourgeois parlor still existed.

Meanwhile, the cupboard problem confronting the living room has been substantially resolved. It continues to exist, but in an attenuated form, harmless like a cold in comparison with a case of flu, with dissolved fronts and plenty of wall. Nor is the living room a setting for self-display any longer, having instead become a temporary multipurpose-work-fun-multimedia space. The scene of battle has retreated to the bedroom, where the wardrobe traditionally finds its place as well. Raging there is a battle for storage space, down to the square centimeter, with each given article of clothing – a blouse or a purse, a pair of shoes or a three-piece suit – struggling to find its place.

Persia in Gelsenkirchen

Alongside the wall cabinet and the sideboard, the Persian carpet was an emblem of superior domestic culture, certifying taste and cosmopolitanism – and for some, a desirable financial investment as well. No longer. Clicking through online sales portals, we find that "100% genuine, hand-knotted" silk carpets can easily be acquired by the ton in a single evening. Dangling before prospective buyers are marvelous examples, splendid patterns, and delectable color combinations. Some are even listed as "very clean," and guaranteed to come from homes without smokers or pets. All for naught. Even established businesses in city centers struggle to draw buyers with slashed prices, clearance sales, and store closures. What happened? Clearly, the good old Oriental carpet has lost its value and prestige. This has little to do with its knot density or aesthetic qualities. Anyone who has walked across a naked floor on a winter's day and then stepped onto a Persian rug knows all too well how a carpet insulates against cold, even improving the overall indoor climate subjectively. Sunlight, moisture, carpet beetles, and aggressive vacuum cleaners: the enemies of the quality Oriental carpet are legion. Then there are house pets, as showcased inimitably by Gerhard Polt in his dog sketch: "No, Hindemith, get off the Persian!" And this prize possession has evidently never recovered. Just Google the search term "Persian carpet," and the term "suburban" pops up automatically. Such adornments are associated with the generation that liked to haul back such articles from holiday trips – sometimes even two or three of them. For interwoven with every carpet, in the end, was a vacation anecdote, one that always began with "Do you remember?" Amazing, what the words "Persian carpet" still trigger. But it makes no difference: as the number of overseas travels balloons, the desire for Oriental carpets subsides. Strange, actually; they seem perfect for the current lounge culture. Not by accident, a Persian proverb reads: "Wherever thy carpet lies is thy home." Perfect for an age of residential nomads, who hurriedly plug in a toothbrush while thrusting a notebook under one arm, but still lack access, apparently, to a flying carpet.

Cheerful Collage

These days, we experience a cheerful collage, one that tolerates much, including the contradictory. The designer Kilian Schindler demands one thing of a living room: "Life!" He concedes that tomorrow, furnishings and other domestic elements will not differ radically from those of today. It is instead a question of emphasis and of materials. "Kitchens and living areas are progressively merging," he predicts, "the sofa is evolving into a space-filling and space-articulating relaxation zone." And because he loves direct exchanges between people, he expects furniture designed to contain entertainment technology to shift away from the focus of attention. Schindler's world is plural in character, and it offers space for personal statements, for mixtures of vintage and high-tech, adapting itself to new circumstances: "When friends come to dine, the table is extended, the sofa ousted." The table, or perhaps simply the "board," is simply a must: from now on, let's simply refer to it as the living, family, and friend room. And the furnishings of such a free space are as manifold as its appellations. A space in a perpetual state of change requires no cohesive set of furnishings that wear out over time and require replacement as an ensemble. Not long ago, people bragged about not owning a single piece of used furniture. Today, the trip to the vintage shop is a well-established Saturday afternoon ritual. A living space, hence, can accommodate many different things: shelving and toy chests, monitors and assemblages of chairs. On view now is a variegated collage that is a major fun factor.

If the living room was once characterized by heavy furniture and rigid rules, it has gradually become a place deserving of the name. The off-the-rack living room that still haunts the brochures of some furniture wholesalers is now obsolete, along with the wall cabinet and the TV armchair. Now, life strides in and sits at a long table with a group of friends who mingle with the family. And since large lofts remain unaffordable for most, we make do with smaller rooms, which become cozy and convivial by way of compensation. Of course, all of this sounds too good to be true, but obviously, the living room has long since become an arena of urban adventure and wish-fulfillment. And in the absence of the old thought prohibitions, and given a multiplicity of possibilities, from which each of us can pick and choose freely, words are coming back into use that were long confined to our grandparents' vocabularies, expressions from which an entire generation sought to distance itself: "The parlor," remarks the Munich architect Sebastian Kofink: "is a room where people meet, where anything can take place." Exactly. Everything is possible in the new "best room." It remains to be seen when and how the housing sector responds to altered living habits with new floor plans.

Apartment Viewing

Building blocks and game pieces litter the bed and floor. Teddy bears and dolls are entangled in the corner as though engaged in a wrestling match. Proceed with caution! Every step is dangerous, and could land you in an ambulance! Chaos in the child's bedroom is probably the commonest of clichés – but necessarily false. Who still maintains order within the few square meters known as the child's bedroom? Anyone who has children knows: the entire apartment is a playground – with Mommy and Daddy serving at times as hapless play figures.[16]

Going wild in the children's bedroom? Mainly, it's the fault of parents who won't listen to reason when it comes to accoutrements for little ones. Everything absolutely must be bright and natural, practical and versatile – and of course utterly special. Nothing is too extravagant for the rising generation. Young princesses and princes acquire everything their parents yearned for during childhood, most of it formerly unattainable: pedal cars, Carrera model trains, canopy beds, silk curtains. These days, a peek into a child's bedroom exposes the souls of the parents: glimpsed here between furry teddy bears and laser swords, dolls and board games are ancient desires and dreams, which have now, finally, assumed concrete form.

A classic is the canopy bed for little princesses, together with all kinds of add-ons – from the bed cave to secret compartments, and all the way to seasonal fabrics. Even ordinary beds can be converted into genuine canopy beds via extensions. And the bed itself is the most changeable ingredient in the childhood cosmos. Now the single bed, now the bunk or loft bed: there are fora and information exchanges for all of them, with individual products put through their paces and critiqued. The central point is a healthy environment. No other topic is the subject of such passionate debate as paints and varnishes, the vapors emanated by various materials, their ecological balance sheets. Exceptionally popular are products derived from sustainable forestry. And of course, everything should be safe, stable, and last at least a few years.

Discussions of merchandise are exhaustive, and inevitably arrive at the melancholy observation that no matter how painstakingly natural the child's environment is, she will end up buying plastic junk with her allowance or acquire it from friends. Can the sustainable lifestyle coexist with such environmental sacrilege? This question is not restricted to wood versus plastic, the healthful versus the fashionable, and will likely be the decisive issue in years to come, one that goes beyond the furnishings of tomorrow.

As a rule, the children's room has no shortage of playthings, and instead lacks space. Hence the demand for convertible sofas and loft beds, along with shrinkable and expandable furniture like seating cubes, which should moreover survive the initial school years. Luigi Colani's flexible desk was already sought after in the 1970s, in conjunction with the appropriate ergonomic chair. Today, expertise is readily available on dozens of websites; the available selection of products has exploded, and the prerequisites for a healthy childhood environment along with it.

Today, the ubiquitous marketing of childhood through theme worlds and brands has become oppressive. Could anyone avoid the megatrends of recent decades, from Star Wars to Harry Potter? All of the unavoidable merchandising articles and accessories, from mobile phone sheaths to game figures, and all the way to complete costumes? In 2019, according to Statista, toy manufacturers transacted circa 90 billion US dollars in business worldwide, with the usual suspects leading the pack: Lego, Mattel, Hasbro. In Germany alone, revenues rose in 2019 to circa 7.7 billion euros, with growth rates in particular for action figures (+17.4%) and dolls (+12.5%), while cuddly toys were less in demand. In view of these numbers, it hardly seems surprising that vendors such as Kaufland actually advise "restricting the number of toys in the child's room to a minimum," since a surfeit of playthings interferes with the child's development: "It is vital that the [child] remain occupied with a toy for an extended period of time, allowing it to enter into her fantasy world." No specialist in pedagogy could have said it better. Quality, not quantity. Increasing in dimensions together with the accumulating mountains of toys are critiques of such, and in particular of the marketing and digitalization of childhood.

Multimedial Upgrading

Here, there is some good news: some devices are no longer seeing rising sales: record players and Walkman are at most curiosities, CD players and ghetto blasters consigned to the scrap heap. Instead, there are Bluetooth loudspeakers, which can stream podcasts, audio plays, and music – not to mention mobile terminal devices of all kinds: iPads and smart phones are jacks-of-all-trades. By 2017, according to statistics supplied by the digital association Bitkom and by Statista, circa 15% of first graders already owned their own tablet, and for children eight to nine years of age, it was already one-third. Older children must choose between a cell phone and a television, with 37% of fourteen-year-olds owning the latter. These numbers are of course only snapshots, and change from year to year. What remains is the disquieting sense that our access to the world has shifted from the touching and grasping of objects to the swiping of digital surfaces. At the same time, the age of entry into the digital world is growing younger all the time: some two-year-olds are already app experts who casually instruct their perplexed grandparents. But the high-tech nursery has its downside. Suddenly, "voice operated dolls and cuddly toys with cameras, smart watches and smart pacifiers, surveillance and diaper apps" become gateways for unwanted data collectors, as the German Federal Agency for Civic Education has warned. It becomes difficult to strike a balance between the justified desire to give kids a good start on the Internet, and the need to develop their capacities in an all-embracing way, or at least to offer them decent choices. At stake is not an either/or, not about pitting tailoring, carpentry, and handicrafts against swiping and chatting, and the answer must instead be inclusive. For the digital world of tomorrow too will require a tangible connection with the material realm, as fragile as the bridge between the two now appears.

Undiminished in any case is the incredible capacity of children to invent their own fantasy worlds. The bedsheets become a cave, a chair a portal into another, more exciting universe. The most marvelous adventures take place in the imagination – and up to the present, the boss is still called Mommy, who stands in the doorway at some point, reminding the young warriors and space travelers that it's time to tidy up and do some homework. A temporary victory at best. Pretty soon, a "Do Not Enter" sign hangs on the door, and at the least with puberty, the cards are completely reshuffled anyway.

Apartment Viewing

The Semi-Public Space:
The Bedroom

For a long time, this door remained tightly shut. Even during apartment tours, it would be opened just a crack, granting guests a brief glimpse of the inner sanctum before being closed again. Despite 1968 and various liberating tendencies, the middle-class bedroom remained as private as ever. Lying at the end of the corridor, an oasis of quiet, a cul-de-sac in the home floor plan. No more. The bedroom is no longer a place of shamefaced retreat for intimate partners where your parents withdrew, switching off the light: it has transformed into a nonchalant space of self-display. The main thing is a large, comfy bed where guests are welcome, sprawling comfortably alongside their hosts.[17]

The new bedroom is open to all, inviting the casual display of bodies and community. The pajama party has now become a clever mixture of calculated self-display and adroit self-marketing. Those who post everything about themselves can hardly exclude intimate aspects. In bed with friends, a new way of celebrating the day. And why not? The former sleeping place for committed couples has come to resemble a comfortable place to lounge, and has been shifted toward the center of the apartment, favored with a combination of giant monitor, walk-in wardrobe, and adjoining bathroom.

In 1922, Le Corbusier, the godfather of modernism demanded: "Do not change your clothes in the bedroom. It is highly unpalatable, and gives rise to a displeasing disorder." Dressing, according to Le Corbusier should take place in a room adjoining the bathroom, which incidentally should be one of the largest in the home, like the parlor in earlier times: "If possible, with a wall consisting of nothing but windows that looks onto a terrace for sunbathing." This type of openness, with its sweeping views, exists today on monitors and cell phones – the sensation of being connected with the outside when in one's own apartment, even more: a part of the whole.

Apropos here is a word that has belonged to the homeowner's vocabulary for years now. The master bedroom. The name is suggestive of the lordly claim, so to speak, of taking possession of and maintaining sovereignty over the remainder of the house. The land is in search of such prominent places. First and foremost, they require space (and in the layouts of today's new apartments, good interior architects). Nothing embodies this change like the box spring bed, familiar from television series and a few (US-)luxury hotels. Sleep experts and some senior citizens swear by the enhanced reclining comfort of this classic, consisting of an innerspring mattress with topper. But comfort here is not solely a function of depth, but of width as well: the 140 cm queen-sized bed yields now to the French bed, with its 160 cm and a single mattress – which is in turn supplanted by the king-sized bed, 2 m in width. People are growing simultaneously larger and older, according to statistics. Accompanying the fashionable box spring bed are various layers, coverings, and cushions – transforming the sleeping place into a piece of representative furniture that stands in the midst of life, and in the middle of the room. A cuddly, showy talent that easily outshines the built-in wall cabinets that surround it. So much for the new bed culture, so reminiscent of the sensual pleasures of the court, its brocade and embroidery, before the bourgeois revolution relegated the state bedroom to a private retreat. Approximately two hundred attendants gathered around Louis XIV during his morning toilet – today, there are fans instead. Both monarchs and public personalities reigned from their beds, like Yoko Ono and John Lennon, whose legendary "Bed-In" of 1969 was a minor sensation. Surely, their king-sized bed would hardly suffice for today's celebrities, who nonchalantly swirl private and public together while wearing pajamas.

Pillow Talk

When it comes to beds, the Germans like it hard. At least when it comes to mattresses. Under the covers, however, things are changing: suddenly, mattresses are hip, and can be ordered online. Our beds are becoming increasingly sophisticated. Not that it's easy to get a good night's sleep in our 24-hour information society.[18]

They must be replaced every ten years, experts advise. At the least. No, not your bed partner, but what is found underneath: the strata that make a bed a pleasant place for a night's repose: the mattress. Spring core or cold foam? Hard or soft? A trial phase lasting one hundred days, or an on-the-spot decision? Allergy-proof or standard? Latex or pocket spring mattress? Reversible mattress with summer and winter sides, perhaps with horsehair, hand-sewn?

Advocates can be found for all of the above, possibly for good reasons. But what is the best, the most fashionable, the most appropriate? These may turn out to be three very different questions. Earlier, things were simpler. When spring core and cold foam were more or less standard. And everything else a luxury, or simply unavailable. Meanwhile, you would need a degree in bedology just to review your options, to say nothing of the hype about mindfulness and electronically monitored, healthful (or less debilitating) sleep.

The bed has become political. Show me your app, and I'll tell you who you are. Or hope to become. At least between 11 PM and 7 AM. All of a sudden, how much – or little – you sleep is a topic of conversation. And you need a good night's sleep to listen to someone blathering on about how "four hours suffice." Not everyone is a Napoleon. While books on healthy sleep, the midday (or power) nap, on how to fall asleep (the motto being: every child can do it) have become bestsellers, perpetually new bed systems crowd onto the market. The winner in recent years: the box spring bed.

Some sleeping supports have enjoyed a heyday only to disappear, an example being the integrated bed/radio. What happened to all of those futons and waterbeds, the heroes of the 1970s and 1980s? In the end, a futon was much more

Apartment Viewing

than a sleeping surface. It was a commitment. Something for purists who already had everything, and were now on a quest for the essential. They renounced bed frames and steel springs in a search for the genuine sleep experience. For the rest of us, it remained a challenge to the spinal column, inspired by the Far East.

Something similar could be said about the waterbed. Unforgettable, what the James Bond set designer Ken Adam concocted for *Diamonds Are Forever* – a transparent Plexiglas aquarium with five hundred saltwater fish, integrated telephone, and bar. The actors, evidently, were less than thrilled with this love nest. Jill St. John found the bed frame far too cold, while Sean Connery regarded the entire business as suspect. Experts remarked that the chic saltwater bed couldn't possibly function in reality. The anti-algae chemicals alone would have meant the demise of all those pretty fish.

In 1833 the Scottish physician Neil Arnott brought "Dr. Arnott's Hydrostatic Bed" onto the market, designed to spare his patients' pressure sores during extended convalescence. But the construction only achieved genuine popularity in the 1980s. Incidentally, Charles Prior Hall submitted a patent in 1968. The curiously terse description reads: "Liquid support for human bodies." Science fiction author Robert A. Heinlein too was fascinated by a waterbed future, which he characterized accurately: "A pump to control water level, side supports to permit one to float rather than simply lying on a not very soft water-filled mattress. Thermostatic control of temperature, safety interfaces to avoid all possibility of electric shock, waterproof box to make a leak no more important than a leaky hot water bottle rather than a domestic disaster, calculation of floor loads (important!), internal rubber mattress and lighting." Heinlein spoke of "an attempt to design the perfect hospital bed by one who had spent too damn much time in hospital beds."

Over time, the system developed further, from the hard-sided to the soft-sided to the lightweight waterbed. But now, after so much bubbling enthusiasm, a small dose of bad news: such mattresses require heating, something understood, evidently, by the ancient Persians with their goatskin sacks, which they laid in the sun in winter, and filled with fresh spring water in summertime.

But what remains from all of these fashions? Perhaps an awareness that alongside the indispensable bed technologies, the zenith of the online mattress, and the triumph of the box spring bed, a distant relative is flourishing: the sofa bed, which owes its existence to increasingly restrictive floor plans, a shapeshifter that moreover forms a bridge between the (no longer so very) private sphere and the public realm. For one thing is certain: sleeping comfort also depends on the size of the apartment where nocturnal existence takes place.

Everyday Life in the Bedroom

Everyday life, of course, is something else. These days, the dimensions of the typical German bedroom approach those of a prison cell. Recently, a home building firm featured the following dialogue: "The average size of a child's bedroom is $14\,m^2$, while the parents' bedroom measures $16\,m^2$. Is that enough?" The question is justified, even considering the polite response: "It depends upon the layout – off hand, it's hard to say. Our bedroom measures $10\,m^2$, and that's enough for us." Ten m^2, of course, marks the dividing line between a room and a storage compartment. One home expert recommends planning between 12 and $15\,m^2$, including a wall measuring three m in length to accommodate a wardrobe. But what if no more than $10\,m^2$ is available? All that remains is a "recourse to a loft bed,"[19] to cite the title of an article in *taz* concerning rising rent prices that appeared in 2014 – and nothing has changed since then. On the contrary. The bedroom has long since become a kind of final spatial reserve of the apartment, and is being gradually devoured. First, the ironing board finds a new home in the wardrobe, followed by the vacuum cleaner, then the home trainer, and other cardio devices. At some point, the desk wanders in as well. So much for the place where the weary spirit finds a well-deserved repose, and the body claims its space.

Fashion victims know what it's like. At some point, even the largest wardrobe bursts its seams – at the least when pullovers have been compressed into briquettes, and three-piece suits are squashed together so tightly that cleaning and pressing become superfluous. Now, finally, it's time for a walk-in closet. Books can be digitalized, compact discs even more readily, but clothing simply requires space. The first to arrive are the boxes, stacked on top of the wardrobe, or wherever, until the last piece of airspace has been consumed – right up to the ceiling. In the end, only radical solutions remain. The triumph of consumer society is clearly in evidence in the wardrobe. Nearly 20 years ago, Carrie Bradshaw in *Sex and the City* set new standards, surpassed only by Imelda Marcos. Ever since, large wardrobe systems have been obligatory: they grow step-by-step, ultimately conquering the entire bedroom, with their bright fronts and abundant light, which appears as soon as a door is opened.

Bags of lavender are hung to repel moths, objects squeezed in. The doors closed. As Hollywood knows better than anyone, this is where the real adventure begins. The wardrobe is somehow uncanny. It seems capable of opening a door to another dimension, of harboring assorted monsters. It is the perfect cast member for screwball comedies or farces that revolve around mistaken identities – sooner or later, this lover or that one is destined to vanish without delay behind sliding doors.

"You should rent an apartment that is somewhat smaller than the one occupied by your parents," advises Le Corbusier. "Consider the economy of movement involved." Today, apartments are smaller by virtue of necessity, since almost no one can afford an undivided floor of an old-style apartment building. And the bedroom? These days, it takes the form of a mini-office with mini work desk, the digital file cabinet absorbed miraculously into a notebook. Astonishing: rather than simply going to bed, we tend to spend the evening searching for apps designed to optimize sleep. "Reduce sleep, achieve more," in conjunction with the suggestive notion that less sleep is somehow an emblem of success: such recommendations reveal that sleep, and with it the bedroom, reside well within the domain of the self-optimization industry, which now searches for the final reserves of a life that is otherwise thoroughly structured. The place of reproduction and regeneration is dead, long live the self-optimized living space. Upon arising, we lay ourselves comfortably on the bedspread: equipped with notebook, cell phone, and iPad, the bed, shoulder-height backrests at the ready, becomes a fully-fledged workplace.

Twenty years ago, the sociologists Thomas Jung and Stefan Müller-Doohm investigated the bedroom culture of the event society,[20] and diagnosed the "privatization of sleep" and "a bedroom culture permeated by middle-class principles." They identified ten main types of bedroom culture, among them the "ecologically oriented naturalness type," the "creative-avant-garde type," the "multifunctional spatial economy type," the "conventional country-style type," and finally the "exotic transcultural type." It would appear that today, we are all of these, depending upon the time of day.

Little remains of the "separation between public and private spheres" and the "progressively reduced boundaries when it comes to a sense of personal shame." The boundary erosion of the working world has meanwhile brought down the thickest of walls. It appears that the bedroom, formerly "the spatially organized and socially conditioned unity of sleep and coitus," as Thomas Jung and Stefan Müller-Doohm characterize it, has now become a space of reception and display – allowing it to catch up, finally, with the kitchen and the bathroom. Life now becomes public and is enacted in the plural. One strives toward representative grandeur (the bed); another is constrained by efficiency to occupy the smallest possible space. Both versions connect, no longer independent entities, but integrated now into a continuous stream of friends, clicks, and networks.

Apartment Viewing

Green Spaces:
Balcony and Allotment Garden

Located beyond the front door for some time now has been a normal – and for many perhaps the most important – area of the apartment. Every terrace, every balcony, augments real estate value. The functions fulfilled during the 1980s by winter gardens and porch types – zones that oscillated between the almost-outside and the still-more-or-less-inside – are fulfilled today by simpler rooms, especially when urbanites return home from day trips fully weatherproofed: they occupy terraces and balconies, furnishing them like living rooms, and nearly year-round.[21]

Earlier, the balcony embodied the sheer desire (and at times, the unavoidable necessity) of spending the summer at home. The brilliant architect and urban planner Bruno Taut already christened the green area of his Hufeisensiedlung (Horseshoe Housing Estate) in Berlin as the "outdoor living area," planting it with a semicircle of cherry trees. He sought to introduce nature in the minds of city dwellers, erasing the demarcation line between the two zones. His aim was a spirit of community among residents. The outdoor feeling has come into its own, the community feeling at public viewings at least, or else in the beer garden.

What is the origin of the desire to transform one's balcony into a second living room? It doesn't take a degree in sociology to detect here the final reserve of freedom in our regimented, planned lives. People who find themselves perpetually pressured not to miss a single tweet or message nurture the desire for brief timeouts, if only five minutes of peace and quiet on the balcony – which seems tailor-made for the purpose. The way is shown by the city lounges that have thrived for years now: pour sand onto the sidewalk, set up a few lounge chairs, hang colorful lanterns, and you're all set: a beach relaxation zone. Now comes the next logical step, as the Germans fully furnish their balconies and terraces. In demand in particular are elaborate pieces of the kind found in living rooms as well. The market for outdoor furniture shows double-digit growth rates. While reliable data is difficult to come by, the available statistics suggest that Germans spend as much money on outdoor furniture as they do on indoor furnishings: circa 200 euros annually. That doesn't sound like much, but it adds up to billions in revenues.

Sofas, lamps, and even beds are suddenly found out of doors. Some pieces give the impression that the neighbors simply dragged them out of their living rooms. The furnishing of the outdoors began with well-tuned grills, mini-gourmet kitchens on terraces and balconies – a kind of elegant Frankfurt Kitchen, liberated from walls and subdivisions. But with stainless steel fronts and oiled, heat-treated spruce. Following the gas-driven comfort kitchen was seating comfort. When life takes place outdoors, as otherwise only during vacation on the Adriatic or in Malle, then let's have all of the amenities. Outdoor collections are meanwhile as weatherproof as they are presentable. They could as easily sit in a living room as on a terrace. And why freeze your feet on long summer evenings? Many manufacturers have begun to offer weatherproof carpeting as well. Too much sun? There are bed islands with adjustable awnings. Isn't that exactly what the revolution promised? "Brothers, to the sun, to freedom,"[22] sang the workers, and not just at the conclusion of SPD conventions after World War II. The yearning for the light was birthed in the rear courtyards of Berlin's tenements – and modernism delivered, preferably in ways that could be enhanced photographically. An example is the dormitory of the Bauhaus in Dessau, whose tiny outdoor seats served as little places of display before the eyes of the outside world – or stylized diving platforms for leaping into a new society, one that would leave staleness and narrowness far behind. The historic city knew nothing of balconies, which were too loud and sticky anyway; preferred were loggias facing the cool interior courtyard.

Meanwhile, balconies are among the basic amenities of every apartment. Three out of four Germans have a balcony or a terrace. They are in such demand that housing associations go to great expense to upgrade their properties with projecting constructions in hot galvanized steel. The cost of adding a balcony should not be allowed to get out of hand. This point is illustrated by the rent increases that follow such conversions, and by the divergent expert opinions concerning whether a percentage of the balcony surface should be counted as part of the rental space.

The Landscaping Megatrend

More and more people yearn to see vegetation at their doorsteps, have a yen for cultivating and harvesting their own greenery before dropping happily into a recliner. According to the German Federal Institute for Research on Building, Urban Affairs, and Spatial Development, this new passion for gardening reflects "a growing need for greater engagement with nature and environmental protection, and a desire to use green and open areas in dense population centers in particular as places of recreation and relaxation, to safeguard them and enhance their attractiveness." From gray to green: how better to characterize the shift from the car-friendly metropolis with broad lanes leading toward the landscape beyond the city to a city of citizens and participants?

The new guiding principle is simple: take matters into your own hands, live closer to nature. Nurtured today, encouraged by urban gardening and sustainable lifestyles, are older ideals of self-provisioning, as promoted by the Bauhaus, for example. For many, the very first zucchini or carrots that spring up in the home garden are a source of genuine delight. And no one finds it odd that this little paradise is thoroughly artificial. After all, urbanites never hesitated to descend upon parks or public gardens set along motorways after a hard day's work, or to relax on the riverbank in full view of a power plant. Those who cannot find real nature in the city are inclined to delight in a bit of green wherever it is found. Here, the garden is a marvelous alternative, almost a declaration of independence from the walled-in daily routine. In a very different league is the garden house that serves as a home office, and the triumph of the dacha. For stressed-out urbanites, the allotment garden[23] has meanwhile become a genuine place of local recreation, perhaps the last remaining generally accessible utopia after the outdoor swimming pool. Between shrubbery and flower beds, half the city meets here and works collectively, albeit some exclusively for themselves. Laborers and brainworkers, retirees, single parents and family men relax peacefully through the sweat of their brows. Philistines my foot! Even houseplants have experienced an amazing renaissance.[24] Meanwhile, a relic of the 1960s, with monster leaves, which goes by the name of *Monstera deliciosa,* is being lovingly cultivated, and freed of dust and grime for appearances on Instagram. The love of nature – something often taken for granted more by urbanites than country crawlers, who watch their lawn robots roll across the lawn and occasionally allow the buzz saw to sing in order to replenish their fireplaces.

The homemade sourdough, the homegrown tomatoes on the windowsill, and the home-canned tomatoes from last fall are having an impact. Observed in allotment gardens are not just rare butterflies, but also intellectuals and creative workers, who are not above burying their hands in mulch in the hope of a good harvest of pumpkins and carrots. Much has changed in central European garden colonies. Ten years ago, the average age of a subscriber was 60, just under retirement age, while today, around half of the new leases are taken by families. Nearly two in three of these new lessees are younger than 55. Hipsters lend a hand to veterans, children run riot on the lawn. These new faces are transforming our image of garden colonies. Once regarded as bastions of the petite bourgeois mentality, fortified by bylaws, regulations, mercilessly sheared greenery, mathematically trimmed hedges, and containing pathways, some parcels are now home to an unfamiliar offhandedness. Even NABU (Germany's Nature and Biodiversity Conservation Union) find themselves applauding more unfenced green in the city, and praising the virtues of the old cottage garden. This new approach to nature is emerging from the center of society, and will hopefully make a real difference – and moreover without glyphosate.

According to the Bundesverband Deutscher Gartenfreunde (Association of German Garden Lovers; BDG) there are 905,000 allotment gardens in Germany alone, and they cover a surface of more than 40,000 hectares. That corresponds to more than 100 parks the size of Munich's English Garden. More than five million people currently use these gardens, each measuring 370 m^2 on average. Anyone who has done some weeding realizes what an enormous area that is. Many of the newer parcels, hence, are only half that size.

But the family garden is more than the setting for a new spirit of community; lying at the intersection of the most diverse interests, which do not always survive the antagonism between private idyll and pressures for public utilization, it also possesses enormous potential for urban planning. Meanwhile, there is a growing appetite for converting these urban spare lungs into additional settlement areas. There exists a "growing need for construction potential for housing, infrastructure, and commerce," we read in a study published by the Federal Institute for Research on Building, Urban Affairs, and Spatial Development[25] (BBSR). Evidently, the total stock of allotment gardens has been "slightly reduced," with parcels disappearing "where demand is minimal and vacancy rates are high." In figures: since 2011, circa 6500 small gardens were "sacrificed as surface was rededicated to residential development and infrastructural measures." The study refers to this phenomenon as "usage competition." Rising at the same time – and this is by no means a contradiction – is the number of users for the remaining parcels.

The Green Zone at the Doorstep

People who become annoyed at finicky allotment garden statutes – including prescriptions for how surface area is to be used (one third for the garden house, one-third for recreation, and one-third for fruits and vegetables) – forget that the beginnings of the "Schrebergarten" movement in the nineteenth century was thoroughly didactic, even paramilitary. Just as garden edges were expected to stand in rank and file, the plots were expected to serve purposes of physical training. Society was joined to engage in self-instruction, so to speak. How distant all of that seems today. Allotment gardens are no longer self-contained parcels, but instead parts of a public network of green and outdoor spaces, to some extent with play areas or environmentally important zones such as deadwood zones for insects, birds, and reptiles.

Such a garden changes you. Slows you down. Puts things in perspective. For many, it is a living area in nature with optional family connections and forms of neighborliness that are not exhausted in weekly lawn inspections and philistinism. Perhaps that is the greatest advance fostered by these green areas. Invented or real boundaries between people may simply vanish during a conversation across the fence. On a small scale, the hyperdynamic, fluid urban world returns to its senses. The family garden promises to become a fascinating milieu for sociologists and politicians. Will our collective life succeed, with its indispensable alternation between retreat and involvement, coffee klatsch and hip-hop, helping and chilling? The center of society is reclaiming nature. While the Amazon rain forest burns, the hydrangeas bloom. This could be regarded as hypocritical, as a retreat into a tiny idyll, but that would miss the point: more and more urbanites are getting involved in such green zones, and getting closer toward one another as a result.

At times, there is just a small step from automobile culture to the outdoor society. No need for permanent campers at the edge of town, or elaborately designed work sheds in the garden. Generally speaking, we settle in out-of-doors, creating hybrid spaces, no longer quite apartment, not yet entirely garden: terrace living rooms and balcony islands. Even the most tentative step across the threshold generates connections with the world outside, with neighbors and acquaintances on the street. What does this mean for our society of hobby gardeners and urban gardening fanatics? Furnished balconies and terraces suggest that something is really happening when it comes to ventilating ideas: freedom, equality, flowering season!

Lighting and alarm systems
are top priorities

Energy and climate control

Lighting
23 %

Heating
15 %

Radio controlled sockets
13 %

Consumption meters
10 %

Security

Alarm system
18 %

Video surveillance
16 %

Locking system
2 %

Home emergency call system
2 %

House and garden

Blinds and awnings
11 %

Robot vacuum cleaner
9 %

Garden equipment
8 %

Window cleaning robot
3 %

Apartment Viewing

Still Missing:
Storage Space

High above, down in the depths: basements and attics are becoming precious. Doing the laundry, meeting neighbors, wild basement parties: that was yesterday. Today, the attic is a penthouse, the basement a private spa. And the clutter of the past winds up in an external storage depot at the edge of town.[26] We strive to free ourselves of our burdensome possessions, not always successfully. But one thing is certain: space is lacking in the well-organized apartments of today. Where are all of the guest rooms, housekeeping areas, walk-in closets, and storerooms that flicker across the screen during afternoon programming? In today's optimized two- or three-room apartments, they are simply nowhere to be found. You either shed all of those superfluous objects – or shut them away, American-style, in a self-storage facility.[27] While the space problem is to some extent outsourced, the erstwhile residual and additional surfaces of the roof, garage, and basement are utilized in new ways.

Something is definitely going on with the former functional spaces above our heads and beneath our feet. Basements and attics are being refunctioned and upgraded. This is no simple lifestyle trend, but instead essential. In large cities, very few people can afford to allow space to lie fallow. Then there is technological progress. And the desire for convenience by stressed-out urbanites who, after nine hours in the office, are hardly eager for major cleaning campaigns. The former laundry and drying rooms have been supplanted by the washer/dryer combo. And the attic, which awaits rediscovery amid linens and disused furniture, is exalted into the fully converted attic story, a mini penthouse above the city. The motto here is: the higher, the more elaborate and expensive.

Upstairs and downstairs, attic and basement, have more to do than one ordinarily supposes. This doesn't just apply to the British upper classes, whose members occasionally speak as coarsely as any coachman. In the house, the extreme ends long served as reserve areas, where whatever would fit there was stashed, locked away, set to one side. In many cases, just what lurked beneath piles of linens, drawers, and chests came to light only when the remnants of entire generations surfaced after the death of a wealthy aunt. Basement and attic constituted the memory of a place, cubic meters of a now irretrievable past, whether packed in boxes or old moving crates, or simply strewn about indiscriminately. All of this might well be a thing of the past. The thoroughly rationalized apartment and the optimized house make such spatial profligacy inconceivable. "The basement in our apartment building is crammed with storage compartments, while in the attic, thanks to new fire regulations, a yawning emptiness prevails," declares the architect Christian Zöhrer. Storage space must therefore be rented – not right around the corner, perhaps, but nonetheless conveniently situated. Everything else is discarded. Until recently, old furniture and articles of clothing were disposed of at flea markets; today, they can be listed profitably on vintage portals. Which has the ring of efficient business practices, with the bonus of improved mental health. Home life is slimming down. Anything lacking immediate usefulness – anything dubious – is unceremoniously ejected. In opposition to all of this, Christian Zöhrer points out that "basements and storage spaces can be regarded as spaces of the unconscious, where things sink into forgetfulness, but may also rise to the surface of everyday domestic life." The Munich native rejects the total functionalization of dwelling, claiming: "Essentially, these spaces belong to the space of habitation, their significance cannot be appraised too highly. External storage depots fundamentally alter their significance through a loss of direct spatial contact."

Cellar Master, Cellar Spirit, Basement for Parties

These days, it has vanished from sight, the basement for parties. It served as a club sans bouncer, cheap, authentic, and with no closing time. Here was a bit of direct democracy for the kids of the 1970s and 1980s, who couldn't afford a real club, or were too young, or lived too far away and didn't know anyone with a car. An informal location for an evening, with everyone bringing their own alcohol, or raiding dad's cases of beer and larder. While Derrick or Ilja Richter's disco music played upstairs in the living room, the really hot discs were spinning in the party basement, which had been upgraded at some point before the elders had lost interest in the underground, unofficially ceding these few square meters to the youngsters.[28]

The quirky family party basement was more than a noisy, stuffy belowground space that constantly reeked of oil (because the garage was set above it, or the heating system was adjacent). It was a cult, plastered with posters and growing-up stories. But what was obligatory there – aside from as many friends as possible? Rummaging through outdated decorating tips, you encounter the inevitable disco ball, along with cushions and mattresses, and finally an integrated unit consisting of counter, barstools, and beer tap, completed by wall tattoos and soundproofing. But the result wasn't quite so professional: the party basement always looked improvised, the walls casually clad in spruce wood, the floor covered with carpet scraps. And even when exceptional efforts were made, the decor was incidental. The basement was a place to disappear into. The adolescents vanished from their parents' field of vision – they were usually glad to have the house to themselves for a while. The party basement became a place of longing. Here with your own music, drinks, and flirting, you felt somehow grown up. It was a bit like *Catcher in the Rye*, reduced now to German DIN dimensions.

But as a rule, the basement brats of the 1980s didn't actually mastermind things themselves, but instead inherited whatever was already there, Why, however, did an entire generation of hobby craftsmen convert their own basements, decorating them with homemade plywood paneling and wall paintings of exotic elsewheres? Was it really just about gleaning a few moments of happiness on Friday evenings with friends and family? And was the space below ground level really there in order to listen to music undisturbed or to hang with friends? One explanation for this excessive love of the underground is offered by Heinz Bude in his "Sociology of the Party."[29] Bude explains the fervor for subterranean parties with reference to a war generation, drilled for survival, which now, between bar and boiler room, attempted to "work through the still relatively recent experience of aerial warfare. [...] Living on in the party basement was the air raid shelter as a place of extreme community cohesion under the threat of death." Later, the latent menace of death abated, while "extreme socialization" persisted, accompanied now by alcohol and other inebriants.

But at some point in the 1990s, the party cellar ceased to play a role. People preferred being outside in the open air or frequenting hip locations. But the cellar was only finished for good when 2006 the abduction of the underaged girl named Natascha Kampusch came to light and in 2008 the crimes of Josef Fritzl. Today, the basement still exists, of course, but only as a handy storage space. There, old notebooks and worn-out hiking equipment rot together, while the kids engage in combat at Wi-Fi parties.

All the same, memories of wild parties are somehow imperishable. In one online guide, the party basement is referred to as a dream, a place where you can "go wild, spend the evening playing videos games, have a few drinks." Sounds like the land of milk and honey. Except that here, someone has to clean up later on.

Repressed and Buried:
The Basement as a Locus of Psychology

Let's not overburden the basement with meaning – all the same, it's intriguing to note that classical psychoanalysts such as Freud and Jung invoked the image of the house in order to descend into deeper psychic layers. Deposited into the metaphorical basement of our unconscious and subconscious is everything that finds no available space above – which is to say in the reflective strata of consciousness – or has simply been repressed. Stacked up in Freud's cellar are anxieties and impulses, while Jung jokes that consciousness doesn't dare venture down into the basement. Ulrich Seidl does exactly that in his documentary film *Im Keller* (In the Cellar). The director led us into the abyss in 2014, just when the dungeons and perverse counterworlds were coming to light in Strasshof and Amstetten. "There, down below, you – men, family fathers, housewives, married couples, and children – can be who you want," explained Seidl.

Earlier, the cellar was a good place for potatoes, wine, and a workshop. Little is left of all of that, perhaps the wine, unless it rests in a perfectly calibrated wine refrigerator alongside the side-by-side freezer-refrigerator. "Today, standards have risen considerably. Conceivable here for builders, increasingly, are full-fledged recreation rooms," says Gianfranco Maio of MAIOMAIO Architekten.

The unstoppable advancement (and expansion) of the attic and the dramatic upgrading of the basement from residual surface area to wellness and living zones demonstrates that prices per square meter determine how we live, love, and think. Kolja Winkler, an appraiser specializing in moisture damage not only recommends the reliable waterproofing of the basement, but also points out that the "basement is actually the most affordable living space." Winkler calculates that a finished basement enlarges living space up to "50%" – at a fraction of the cost of an added story. A comparable bonus in living space is otherwise achievable only by building an addition, which is often not permitted. In the country, more and more functions are finding their place belowground alongside heat pumps and pellet silos (we are sustainable, after all) which would otherwise be reserved for the upper stories. Found alongside the traditional hobby room are workstations or even self-contained apartments. And the basement sauna (which sits by preference on the roof in northern countries, for the sake of the landscape, the fresh air, the sensation of expansiveness) is upgraded to a wellness station. A space that, as a party basement with bar, displayed at least a whiff of anarchy, receives an upgrade now in both functionality and convenience. The yardstick is the well-equipped hotel, organized entirely around our desires and expectations. The cellar, once characterized primarily as a functional zone (supply storage, laundry room, garage) is obsolete – even the dirty oil heating has been supplanted by the functional ecopower plant; all that is left is to convert the hobby room into an official workstation.

One can only wonder at the efficiency streamlined "factory for living" known as the city. Just as in the economy, untapped reserves are identified and turned to good use. The new basement is not some sort of stuffy souterrain apartment, but can instead be a high-quality living- or workspace. Or a private fitness oasis. The more comfort that is introduced into these formerly residual areas, the more technology, the more they will be missed: spaces that formerly remained somehow undefined, indeterminate.

Relic of the Car-Friendly Society:
The Garage

The garage is not the most illustrious among building tasks. Unlike the bathroom as a place of purification or the kitchen as the heart of family life, it is difficult to elevate functionally. The very name evokes images of open carports through which the wind whistles, or gray prefabricated boxes set along row houses of equal dullness. Enjoying an astonishing ascendancy in contrast is the former horse stable: from a place to store tires and automotive accessories, it has evolved into a fully-fledged component of the home, at least in Berlin, Stuttgart, Düsseldorf, and Singapore. There, cars are meanwhile parked in their own loggias – directly adjacent to the kitchen and the sofa landscape. Nowhere else is the segregation of urban life displayed so explicitly. Those with no desire for small talk and tedious encounters with neighbors can drive their cars directly into the freight elevator, landing directly in the apartment. The vehicle itself becomes a designer object, an expression of refined taste.[30]

Of course, there is also a counter-reaction: apartment and parking space lose their importance. They no longer share the same building, nor even the same street: now, the car stands in a local parking garage. Some urbanites are dispensing with car ownership altogether. Sharing is fashionable, along with short-term rentals, which can be parked anywhere. A practical solution for people who don't want to be tied down, especially to a "stationary vehicle" which, according to statistics, stands around unused 23 hours every day. Of course, this impacts the design of parking spaces. For there is nothing attractive about the garage as such. It sits alongside the building, like the horse stables of yore, or below ground level. You press a remote, the door swings open, the lights switch on. Two minutes later, you enter the elevator with (or without) your purchases. A belowground parking space is a cast-concrete monument to our mobility culture: an expensive shrine for automobiles. And those who hit upon the idea of using the garage differently, perhaps as a storage space for mountain bikes, skis, and boxes, will be quickly reminded by the property management that only cars are allowed here.

In the city, a parking space is still part of the apartment, although it now costs as much an ordinary car once did; it is also vitally important if an owner-occupied apartment is to be resold at some point. And in large cities, depending on location and amenities, those who lease parking spaces pay an impressive monthly fee. Prices are a reflection of shortages. In cities, there are simply too few parking spaces, although in some high-density areas, they account for up to 40% of all circulation areas.

Does the garage reflect the state of our civilization? We are more mobile than ever before, and regard ourselves as more open and egalitarian. In 2012, astonishingly, twice as many cars were registered by men as by women. Experts conclude that looking ahead to the year 2030, women will play a greater role in automobility. The same is true of older people. Extending these ideas, we can envision the garage too evolving from drab functionality into a multifunctional space: barrier-free and well-lit, practical and networked. Some carports have long since become pergolas and mini sports areas, with some large-capacity garages being transformed into ecogarages, complete with rainwater dispensers, solar cells, and green roofs. The next step would be installing a solar module with storage system on top, converting the entire thing into an "electric fuel station." On the other hand, in view of today's increasingly bulky vehicles, large-capacity garages will be in increasing demand, "with breadths up to 7.5 m and lengths of up to 9 m." Despite winning a prize, the oval designer garage ultimately resembles nothing so much as a banal relic of post-modernism. Garage design is however seeing some genuine movement: reduced fronts and clear proportions engender greater harmony between garage and home. While some are opening up new design spaces, others say adieu to oil spots on the floor and spare fuel canisters, switching to an Elektroflitzer, unsealing the floor, making do with the humble carport. The "fully-serviced garage vehicle" is a dying breed. Many city dwellers instead lease cars only sporadically. They no longer cultivate a libidinous relationship with locomotion on four wheels, instead using an app that divulges the exact location of the nearest available vehicle. Then it's off to the DIY store or furniture showroom, and a couple of hours later, the car is deposited unceremoniously somewhere at the edge of town.

In 1992, in his grandiose novel *The Discovery of Heaven*, Harry Mulisch writes: "A motorist is not a pedestrian in a car but a totally new creature, made of flesh, blood, steel, and gasoline. They are modern centaurs." The subterranean garage still forms the basis of our mobile society. But it need not remain so. Car-sharing and taxi apps, even service providers like Uber, are just the beginning. Soon, when it is mainly self-driving autos that cruise through the streets, the owners will perhaps become small-scale taxi enterprises whose vehicles are perpetually on the move, and no longer require parking spaces. Conversely, we will only use mobility resources when we really need them. The old-fashioned parking garage will become obsolete. It will find its final resting place in luxury apartments, directly alongside the freestanding cooking island and the wellness bathroom. All of the other largely car-free parking places can be converted into community gardens – and garages into plantations for growing mushrooms. Or storage space for boxes filled with all the things we order online.

What we expect from a smart home

Cleanliness thanks to robot vacuum cleaners
79 %

Fresh coffee to wake up
72 %

Automatic call functions
68 %

Crispy roasts in the intelligent oven
48 %

Door openers for parcel deliverers and workman
27 %

Childcare
12 %

Apartment Viewing

Invasion of the Workstations:
The Home Office

As a result of the COVID-19 pandemic, things that modernity had painstakingly segregated collided again abruptly. After the living kitchen and the semi-open-plan bedroom with its wellness bathroom, the home office represents the third turning point in early twenty-first-century domesticity. People, cities, and residences are still adapting to the change. The wider implications of this compulsory solitude in front of the home computer are already being addressed in various sociological and psychological studies. We can only speculate about the results. Depending upon individual circumstances, presumably, such isolation can be experienced as liberating, as a pleasant change, or as penal servitude, to be served out, eight hours a day, in one's own digs.[31]

The putative freedom involved is often illusory. Digital surveillance and constant availability undermine the inviolability of the domestic space. To close the office door, return home, and become a human being again: that was then. Actually, the COVID pandemic only accelerated a tendency that was already observable in recent years. A home office also means that even lunch breaks are not quite so simple to organize. At any moment, something important may intervene, a colleague may request assistance, a superior may demand to see an overdue report. What is to be done? Politely decline? Ostentatiously shove a sandwich into your mouth during the chat? Questions of etiquette are not insignificant. Behind them lurks a more important question: is the home office today a penance or a privilege? From the perspective of a mechanic, who has never had a choice about where to assemble automobiles, working at home is undoubtedly a great boon. A survey by the public opinion research operation Civey conducted for the German Association for the Digital Economy (BVDW) in March of 2020 registered an overwhelming majority in favor of working at home: 58% of the one thousand people questioned "expressly wanted it, while 17.4% remained undecided."[32] This may change once the crisis becomes a permanent condition, and the home office the covert standard. Paid like regular employees, but managing working hours like freelancers? Not all office workers dream of that. Together with places and times, categories too are becoming blurred.

The home office is a challenge – sociologically as well as in design terms. At the interface of home and work, it is a place where worlds collide and clash. And as much as the office has acquired a veneer of coziness in recent years, becoming somehow casual, it nonetheless remains an ersatz home with a temporary ersatz family. Nothing against that, but is the home office a genuine design task? Or instead a question of psychology? The central concern is a sense of well-being, but also a desire for interaction outside of the nuclear family or partnership. Here, the survey results are contradictory. Although nine out of ten questioned "want to be fully or partly mobile regarding their workplaces," as shown by a study conducted in the spring of 2021 by the Boston Consulting Group, The Network, and the job portal StepStone, and involving 208,000 people,[33] a concurrent survey of 28,000 people concluded that only 4% wanted to "renounce the office altogether."[34] Whether or not this represents a genuine contradiction, one thing is certain: the invasion of work time into the home environment alters our perceptions. Familiar certainties perish, new routines take shape – often to the detriment of domestic tranquility.

Evidently, employees are taking advantage of the enforced distancing of the COVID pandemic to undertake extensive renovations. Walls are painted, floors refinished, wallpaper unrolled. In March of 2020, the Pinterest press team reported that searches for "organize work desk in office" rose by circa 473%. Things were similar for research into matters such as "golden milk," which is to say a turmeric latte (an increase of circa 43%), and fashion areas, that is, for the perfect "home-office outfit" (up 82%). Is it permissible to sit in front of the PC wearing a baggy sweater? Of course. If we're going casual, let's go all the way. Of course, social control via video chat restricts personal laxity considerably. You can also Google the German comedian Mario Barth, who poses the greatest of all fashion questions while feigning a hangover and wearing his bathrobe: Why get dressed at all? Suddenly, clarity emerges: not everyone is a Big Lebowski, who can make a stylish impression shopping in his pajamas. Apparently, self-respect matters in the home office too.

Actually, no one needs tips from experts on how to squeeze even more use into the space between four walls, how to make sketches at the kitchen table, or how to make a digital meeting look good at the coffee table. Nor is it a question of how to use a height-adjustable work desk to maximize performance: at stake here are personal decisions that need not as a rule involve either architects or designers. There are good reasons for this. The flaneur ("promenadologist") and sociologist Lucius Burckhardt once said that objects like flatware, which are endowed with high symbolic value but require minimal inventiveness, are not proper design objects. The same is probably true of the home office. Here, everyone should romp and gambol to their heart's content whenever personal preferences come into play. Then, it's no longer a question of "work 4.0" or of the "new work," and instead of the work-kitchen. Or the bed-computer-room. A perfectly normal bit of home life. So we'd better just make the best of it.

Stay Cool

My home is my office. But what does it mean concretely for the future of the domestic sphere when no one knows any longer exactly where work ends and home life begins? As a semi-public place, one's own four walls acquire hybrid traits, calling privacy as such into question. The potential psychological impact was illustrated already by Billy Wilder's film *The Apartment* (1960). Insurance agent C. C. "Bud" Baxter finds himself estranged from his own apartment, which serves as an occasional love nest for a superior. In the long term, the "un-private-home" is probably more dangerous than everything devised to date by clever ergonomists and interior architects to transform the office environment, which appears increasingly cozy and playful, but is actually being fine-tuned for efficiency. Assuming the home office actually becomes the norm, the home will require active protection from the office.

To adapt one's own apartment armed with workplace regulations and DIN specifications, installing a daylight lamp here, ensuring minimal distances there, points in the wrong direction. Is homework to be banned from the dining room table, reserved now for office work? The home is simply not the place for office norms. Guidelines designed to ensure the well-being of employees should be adapted to the new lived reality, not the reverse. When Mommy or Daddy work at the computer with Baby in a sling, it's not about standards, but instead about minutes. Many find it simply impossible to accommodate family life, work, and friends under a single roof. And for many, it's simply a nightmare. Even in a spacious apartment, a permanent office space is simply an intrusion. Multifunctional furniture, folding worktable, and stackable office storage units are not the solution. Instead, it is high time that the categories work, life, and leisure time be reconceptualized, that new spaces be allocated for them. Many will yearn for new forms of segregation; others will adjust themselves to the progressive hybridization of the world. These solutions may take the form of "bed kitchens" or "cooking offices," "working kitchens" or "bed computer rooms," but what that means precisely will have to be defined by each individual in consultation with family members, friends, and acquaintances who are in many cases making similar adjustments.

1   Walter Benjamin, *The Arcades Project*, Cambridge MA, 2002, p. 865.
2   See also Oliver Herwig, "Mit Schirm, ohne Charme," *Süddeutsche Zeitung*, 28 October 2016.
3   Margarete Schütte-Lihotzky, "Rationalisierung im Haushalt" (1926), in Volker Fischer and Anne Hamilton (eds.), *Theorien der Gestaltung. Grundlagentexte zum Design*, vol 1. Frankfurt am Main, 1999. pp. 169–172.
4   Lukas Farwer, "Lebensdauer einer Küche – alle Infos zur Haltbarkeit," *Focus online*, 30 November 2017. praxistipps.focus.de/lebensdauer-einer-kueche-alle-infos-zur-haltbarkeit_97872.
5   destatis.de/DE/Themen/Gesellschaft-Umwelt/Einkommen-Konsum-Lebensbedingungen/Ausstattung-Gebrauchsgueter/Tabellen/a-haushaltsgeraete-gebietsstaende-lwr.html.
6   See ernaehrungsvorsorge.de/private-vorsorge/notvorrat/vorratskalkulator/.
7   Adolf Loos, "Die moderne Siedlung" (1926), in *Sämtliche Schriften in zwei Bänden*, vol. 1, ed. by Franz Glück, Vienna, 1962, pp. 402–428. Cited from Wikisource. de.wikisource.org/wiki/Die_moderne_Siedlung#Anmerkungen_des_Herausgebers.
8   See de.statista.com/themen/4914/kuechen-moebel-in-deutschland/ see as well de.statista.com/statistik/daten/studie/255167/umfrage/umsatz-der-deutschen-kuechen-industrie/.
9   But see this survey from 2008: de.statista.com/statistik/daten/studie/163620/umfrage/stellenwert-der-kueche-in-der-wohnung-nach-altersgruppen/.
10 Sandra Ahrens, "Wie häufig wird in Ihrem Haushalt gekocht?" de.statista.com/statistik/daten/studie/92/umfrage/haeufigkeit-des-kochens/.
11 Marco Dettweiler, "Heiß und trending," *Frankfurter Allgemeine Zeitung*, 10 May 2021. faz.net/aktuell/technik-motor/technik/moderne-kueche-nachfrage-nach-geraeten-ist-zurzeit-enorm-17330185.html.
12 "Küchentrends 2021," *AMK*, 4 February 2021. amk.de/pressemeldung/kuechentrends-2021/.
13 See also Oliver Herwig, "Zelle, Grotte, Wellness-Tempel," *Süddeutsche Zeitung*, 16 September 2016.
14 See also Oliver Herwig, "Abschied von der guten Stube," *Süddeutsche Zeitung*, 8 July 2016.
15 See Oliver Herwig, "Eigernordwand in Furnier," *Süddeutsche Zeitung*, 24 March 2017.
16 See Oliver Herwig, "Chaos im Kinderzimmer," *Süddeutsche Zeitung*, 10/11 July 2021. sueddeutsche.de/leben/chaos-im-kinder zimmer-aufraeumen-erziehung-1.5343984?reduced=true.
17 See also Oliver Herwig, "Das Ende der Privatheit," *Süddeutsche Zeitung*, 30 September 2016.
18 See also Oliver Herwig, "Bettgeschichten," *Süddeutsche Zeitung*, 23 December 2016.
19 Barbara Dribbusch, Pascal Beucker, "Rückzug aufs Hochbett," *taz*, 11 June 2014. taz.de/Enge-auf-dem-Wohnungsmarkt/!5040382/.
20 Stefan Müller-Doohm, Thomas Jung, *"Kultur und Natur im Schlafraum"*, in: Stefan Müller-Doohm and Klaus Neumann-Braun, eds., *Kulturinszenierungen*, Frankfurt a. M., 1995, pp. 239–262; Stefan Müller-Doohm, Thomas Jung, Ludgera Vogt, *"Wovon das Schlafzimmer ein Zeichen ist. Text- und Bildanalysen von Schlafraumkultur im Werbemedium,"* in: Hans A. Hartmann and Rolf Haubl, eds., *Bilderflut und Sprachmagie. Fallstudien zur Kultur der Werbung*, Opladen, 1992, pp. 245–266; Stefan Müller-Doohm, "Die kulturelle Kodierung des Schlafens oder: Wovon das Schlafzimmer ein Zeichen ist," in: *Soziale Welt*, no. 1, vol. 47, (1996): pp. 110–122. uol.de/stefan-mueller-doohm/publikationen
21 See also Oliver Herwig, "Draußen vor der Tür," *Süddeutsche Zeitung*, 19 August 2016.
22 de.wikipedia.org/wiki/Br%C3%BCder,_zur_Sonne,_zur_Freiheit. See also Julia Haungs, "Radikal anders wohnen – Leben in Bauhaus-Architektur," *SWR2*, 29 June 2020. swr.de/swr2/wissen/radikal-anders-wohnen-leben-in-bauhaus-architektur-swr2-wissen-2020-07-06-100.html.
23 See also Oliver Herwig, "Mit Kürbis und Hortensie trotzen wir dem Chaos," *Neue Zürcher Zeitung*, 26 September 2016. nzz.ch/feuilleton/mit-kuerbis-und-hortensien-trotzen-wir-den-katastrophen-ld.1504728.
24 On this topic, see for example: ndr.de/kultur/Revival-der-Zimmerpflanzen,zimmerpflanzen168.html; ndr.de/ratgeber/garten/zimmerpflanzen/Bogenhanf-Robuste-Zimmerpflanze-im-Retro-Look,bogenhanf102.html.

25 "Kleingärten im Wandel – Innovationen für verdichtete Räume," bbsr.bund.de/BBSR/DE/FP/ReFo/Staedtebau/2017/kleingaerten/03-ergebnisse.html

26 See also Oliver Herwig, "Keller und Dachboden werden edel," *Süddeutsche Zeitung,* 29 July 2016.

27 Compared with the US, the European self-storage market, with only 3247 self-storage locations in 2017, and ca. 8.7 million. m^2 of rentable surface, is just getting started. See de.wikipedia.org/wiki/Mietlager; "Selfstorage." Stiftung Warentest, 10 September 2014. test.de/Selfstorage-So-schaffen-Sie-schnell-mal-Platz-4745489-0/.

28 See also Oliver Herwig, "Freiheit im Untergrund," *Süddeutsche Zeitung,* 11/12 January 2020. See also de.wikipedia.org/wiki/Josef_Fritzl; de.wikipedia.org/wiki/Im_Keller_%282014%29; de.wikipedia.org/wiki/Natascha_Kampusch; party-ratgeber.com/partykeller/; deutschland-feiert.de/partylocation/partykeller.

29 Heinz Bude, "Prolegomena zu einer Soziologie der Party," *Die Welt,* 23 November 2015. welt.de/kultur/article149142953/Prolegomena-zu-einer-Soziologie-der-Party.html. See also z-i-g.de/pdf/ZIG_4_2015_party_bude_5.pdf.

30 See also Oliver Herwig, "Ein schöner Schrein", *Süddeutsche Zeitung,* 30 December 2016; Gerhard Matzig, "Wohnen: Über Garagen und was darin zu finden ist," *Süddeutsche Zeitung,* 2 April 2021.

31 See also Oliver Herwig, "Die Welt nach Corona," *Frankfurter Rundschau,* 9 June 2020. fr.de/politik/raum-zeit-dilemma-13793254.html.

32 bvdw.org/der-bvdw/news/detail/artikel/bvdw-studie-mehrheit-der-deutschen-angestellten-wuenscht-sich-wegen-des-corona-virus-home-office-m/.

33 businessinsider.de/karriere/stepstone-umfrage-wie-arbeitnehmer-in-zukunft-arbeiten-wollen/.

34 "Sehnsucht nach dem Büro. Meldung," *Frankfurter Allgemeine Zeitung,* 10 April 2021, p. C1. Includes a reference to the job portal *StepStone.*

Apartment Viewing

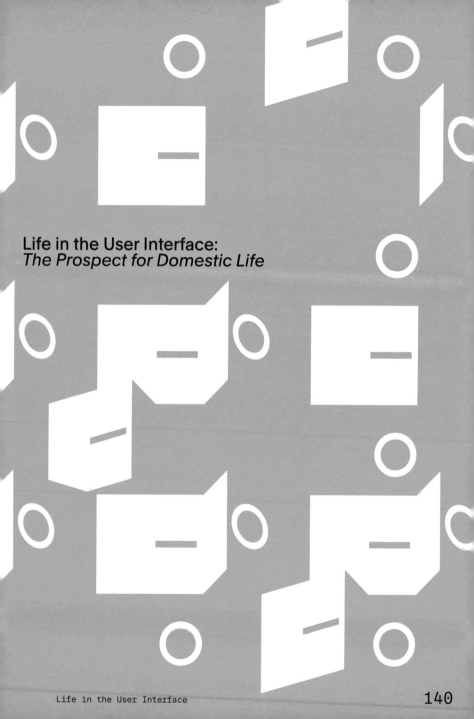

Life in the User Interface:
The Prospect for Domestic Life

The Prospect for Domestic Life

"I actually think most people don't want Google to answer their questions, they want Google to tell them what they should be doing next."[1]

Eric Schmidt,
former Google CEO and
executive chairman

The era of the analog apartment is coming to an end. Soon, it will be a part of a cloud infrastructure that knows quite a lot about the desires and preferences of occupants, and which implements them as a matter of course in profiles, personalized offerings, services, and new business ideas. Big Data opens up a simply endless mine of raw materials, allowing it to distill trends from algorithms. Many answers to the question of how domestic life will look in the future are found in the server farms of Google, Facebook, Apple, and the NSA. An analysis of intrinsically banal but detailed data tells us more about the transformation of user behavior and the thinking of tenants, owners, real estate agents, and builders than many sociological studies. We are already living in the future.

The smart home extends ordinary space into a user surface. But what is emerging now beneath these digital components? In the future, life will be comfortable, fully electrified, interactive – and perhaps rather lonely. Cocooning in one's own filter bubble elicits the need for a countertendency in the public sphere; such reduction necessitates the full breadth of the Web. The overall direction of development remains uncertain. But one thing is certain: the world needs more flexible floor plans. And more community.

A direct path leads from the modernist "machine for living" to the machine living of digital modernism, with its networked kitchen appliances, virtual assistants, and other conveniences that occupy a gray zone between support, surveillance, and round-the-clock service provision. Life in the user interface is continuously "improved" – a promise that seems to be borrowed directly from the modernist avant-garde. But the price for all of this? We move in the digital ecosystems of the individual providers. Users pay by surrendering their data. In exchange, they receive a lifelong better version of the best currently available data worlds.

Before long, the algorithms of AI "know" which lighting mood we prefer when we come home from work, and which playlist helps us to wake up in the morning. Our homes read all of our wishes directly from our own lips. And when someone

The Prospect for Domestic Life

speaks of "wiping," it is not in reference to a dust cloth, but instead to the display on a mobile device that guides lighting scenarios, and will soon replace the front door key.

A study performed by the industry service Bitkom in September of 2020 produced the following results regarding digital accessories: lighting came out in front (23%), before security systems (18%) and video surveillance (16%), heating (15%), electrical outlets (13%), utility meters (10%), and garden equipment (8%). Bringing up the rear were window-cleaning robots (3%), along with locking and emergency call systems (each 2%).[2] Of greater interest is the preferred type of control system: the stationary language assistant (85%) beat the smart phone (74%) – and more than one-half of all users preferred control via voice command (52%). And it certainly is a relief when you have a baby on one arm and have just three minutes to locate a vital document for an impending online meeting. Important as well is the realization that we use smart home apps because they promise "greater comfort and quality of life" (72%), "more security" (65%), and more energy efficiency (52%). All three criteria have risen markedly over the past three years, while fewer people expect to save money as a consequence – from 38% in 2018 to just 24% in 2020.

Comfort is the killer argument. Our blinds are lowered automatically at sunset; we regulate the temperature of our bedroom en route, ensuring coziness upon arrival. Robot vacuum cleaners make the rounds, and Alexa is simply a member of the family, for example when she orders flowers for a birthday we have forgotten all about, yet again.

The Prospect for Domestic Life

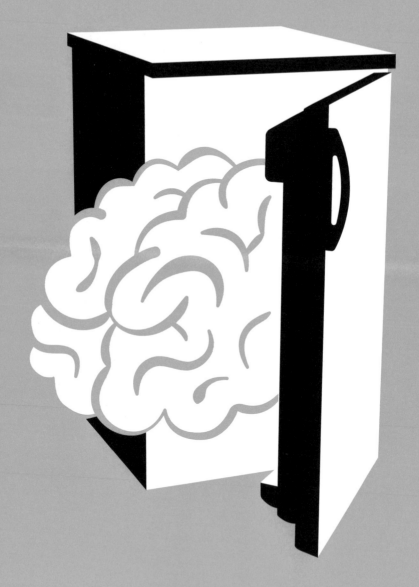

How Smart Should
Your Fridge Be?

Are we still masters in our own homes? This has less to do with Freud, and more with the primal fear of being challenged, outstripped, or even threatened by our own creations: Goethe's "Sorcerer's Apprentice," Mary Shelley's *Frankenstein*, and Isaac Asimov's *I, Robot* have contributed collective images to the intriguing question of the ideal intelligence level of the refrigerator, which, following a software update, orders healthy foods because it has just googled our body-mass index – or perhaps simply hacked it? Or because, thanks to a contractual clause, our hospital is monitoring our food orders. We still derive amusement from Alexa's delectable misunderstandings,[3] when dollhouses are unexpectedly ordered after a TV ad that plays back the signal word "Alexa," yet even such collateral damage just makes us appreciate our solicitous AI all the more.[4] The all-around hassle-free package of the digital economy produces the most efficient form of surveillance – right inside our own four walls. The future may find us defending the boundaries of privacy.[5] The "Internet of Things," with its potential data streams, will certainly not make the task easy.

Considering the aging of our society, it may prove useful to promote the networking of homes and people in a barrier-free environment,[6] with inanimate objects fulfilling social function as helping hands and invisible guardian angels. As early as 2002 David Tonge, a partner of Pentagram Design, designed new services for the then telecommunications giant AT&T: "Pensioner Joe," for example, wears a blood pressure monitor on his T-shirt, while the flatware counts calories, keeping records of everything he eats. "Phyllis," on the other hand, the mother of three children, wears a "personal shopper" on her shoulder bag that not only knows her profile, but also her schedule, and can communicate with goods on the store shelves. It reminds her of things she "might want to consider" for a party that evening, or simply of all the things she "normally" purchases. Steps into a new world to which we have almost adapted ourselves already.

COVID has altered the way we relate to one another, speak, communicate. We Zoom, Skype, and meet at virtual conferences. Anyone who hesitated to use modern contemporary resources before the crisis has been abruptly and

The Prospect for Domestic Life

forcibly updated. Commenting on this rapid shift in April of 2020 was Microsoft chairman Satya Nadella: "We've seen two years' worth of digital transformation in two months. From remote teamwork and learning, to sales and customer service, to critical cloud infrastructure and security – we are working alongside customers every day to help them adapt and stay open for business in a world of remote everything."[7]

In a society where personal encounters have become a rare pleasure, bits and bytes serve to maintain the requisite distance between individuals. The digital becomes standard, and everything else must justify itself. And the next steps seem preordained: the home becomes dissolved into the media universe within which we already operate. Augmented reality is already creating realistic data objects, while walls serve as interfaces – entirely without projectors. The accelerated mediatization of our four walls appears irreversible. We can sacrifice personal libraries, walls, and shelves, but not power outlets or WLAN. "Communism is Soviet power plus the electrification of the entire country,"[8] explained Lenin in 1920: today, dwelling is domestic life plus the digital networking of one's entire life.

The Prospect for Domestic Life

Housing 4.0:
The Home 30 Years from Now

Retina and fingerprint scanners had their heyday in 2028, when an aging society succumbed to a collective mania for security. Nothing seemed more awful than to suddenly forget one's home access code (hello Alzheimer's). Then came the olfactory sensor: invisible, ubiquitous. Not only could it tell who was standing in the elevator at the moment; it also informed health insurance providers if a patient (by then, everyone had become a permanent patient) had failed to conform to her diet plan. Control panels of all types had long since vanished, along with the bumbling domestic robots of the first and second generations, which had whirred through the apartment like beetles gone wild, achieving little more than sweeping up dust under the bed or sofa. Beginning in 2028, it was instead deceptively real simulated house pets that scuttled during the day and hunted for dust and vermin during the nighttime hours. Around 2040, refrigerators and stoves vanished from the home, even voice-operated ones. No one cooked for themselves any longer; instead there were three major delivery services that delivered hot meals at regular intervals together with the daily cocktail of pharmaceuticals. After 2043, anyone who peeled carrots or owned a cooking pot was regarded as a snob. Meanwhile, apartments had become enormous (in the virtual sense, of course), almost infinitely large, and were furnished with commensurate flexibility. First, room-screens dissolved walls, then televisions, olfactory sensors, videogames, and 3D holograms merged to constitute a genuine augmented reality. You could sit in your tiny apartment in Berlin while enjoying a spectacular view of the Mediterranean on Monday, of the Matterhorn on Tuesday, and of the Gobi Desert on the weekend. Thanks to Formplast©, a further development of the 3D printer, articles of furniture emerged as needed from walls and floors, and were melted down again later on. All of a sudden, do-it-yourself home renovating and furniture-making acquired a completely new meaning.

But things got even better: through implants and other enhancements, this ubiquitous technology found its way right into the human body. The distinction between wetware, which is to say DNA-based biology that had emerged through evolution, and hardware, was no longer essential, and instead discretionary. Replacing an absolute boundary line now were fluid transitions. The biosphere and the technosphere coalesced.

Welcome to the future, which will probably look very different from the above sketch. All too often, our perspective

The Prospect for Domestic Life

of the world of tomorrow is little more than a feeble extrapolation of contemporary reality, hopefully somewhat more chic and colorful, wider or slimmer than what is regarded today as incredibly trendy. But trends and tendencies by no means conform to law-like regularities. Otherwise, we would already have flying automobiles (like those conjured in 1932 by Frank Lloyd Wright for his Broadacre City) or atomic vehicles (like the Ford Nucleon of 1958).

The 1950s served as a kind of incubator and experimental laboratory of the future, perhaps even more so than the 1960s, which actually translated a bit of science fiction into reality with the Moon landing. Some projects from that time are reminiscent of visions that enjoy currency today, for example the "House of the Future" of 1957: dimmable lighting that emerges through a polarized plastic ceiling, dishwashers based on high-frequency technology, retractable refrigerated cool zones and microwaves, central air-conditioning (with a few buttons instead of today's control panels), telephones with buttons (instead of the dial) and a hands-free option. And underlying everything, the promise of "utmost convenience and efficiency."

Many such futuristic visions stopped there. They became intoxicated with (and lost themselves in) technological progress, whether of the utopian or dystopian variety – Hollywood has meanwhile produced a disproportionate number of the latter, which are today surpassed on a regular basis by genuine horror headlines: forest fires, catastrophic droughts, storms and flooding that assume shocking proportions. Poverty, climate refugees, and destroyed crops have provided a foretaste of what we and our children can expect if we do not act decisively today. Securing the future demands strenuous effort. Technological and climate changes converge, reinforcing one another. Digital disruption, urbanization, as well as climate change and population growth, in conjunction with a sustained pandemic and large-scale migration, entangle us in ever greater challenges, giving rise to an unresolvable syndrome called uncertainty, which must be confronted not by some politician up there, but instead by all of us.

In the framework of its revised World Urbanization Prospects for 2020, the United Nations Population Division reported that 56.15 percent of world population now lives in cities[9] – a figure that circulated through the media. In the future, the greater part of humanity will reside in urban areas. At the same time, the number of networked devices is exploding: in the consumer area alone, strategists expect around 16 billion such objects by 2030.[10] This amount is double the current world population (currently around 7.7 billion).[11]

Mention of "the future" generally suggests a malleable reality, one that can be consciously altered, guided at least in part; the result of the sum of personal decisions for or against specific variants. But it could turn out very differently. It is perhaps not we who shaped the course of events, but instead, in a perfectly mundane sense, things that steer us. Neither the telephone nor the television, neither the Internet nor the automobile were found on our ancestors' wish lists, and were instead simply imposed on them. Of course, we can select among various brands or colors, but we can hardly choose to live in a flying houseboat or a tire warehouse. With floor plans, things are already becoming difficult. Dwelling remains a conservative matter, defined less by pioneering furniture inventions or radically new residential typologies, and instead by the diffuse field of tension between proximity and distance, comfort and simplicity, the habitual and the exceptional, between the affordable and the slightly out of reach. The designer Raymond Loewy put this in a nutshell most strikingly with his legendary "MAYA" threshold value. He called for products that would be the "Most Advanced. Yet Acceptable."[12] The same is true for dwellings, which will need to do more and more in the future: as emissaries of a world that is as barrier-free as possible, and is maintained in a sustainable fashion.

Dwellings will not become simpler along the interface between societal change and technological disruption. The hybrid home is here to stay. In it, free time and work time are becoming almost impossible to disentangle – and the same is true of intimacy and public life: the one continually conditions the other. While the classical family-centered residence no longer represents the norm, space is opening up for new constellations. Monofunctional rooms have no future and are being supplanted by temporary spaces known as office-bathrooms or living-cooking-bedrooms. The smart home signals a new openness: welcome to the app home! To a domestic realm that is hooked into global data streams and shares our preferences and habits with the Cloud as a matter of course.

In 1927 Kurt Tucholsky poeticized residential and dream spaces under the title "The Ideal" to arrive at a timeless moral: "Everything simple, full of modesty: / Nine rooms – no, let's have ten! / A roof garden, where oak trees stand, / Radio, central heating, vacuum, / Servants, well behaved and silent."

Electronic servants exist already, along with the new cycling domestics, with all of the consequences for a future society. Much about the domestic life of the future may appear alien, but flexible floor plans and new models of community are long overdue. We need more experimentation and greater investment in barrier-free environments – both analog and digital. It rests with us to ensure that this new freedom benefits everyone.

1   Simon Hurtz, "Google will Antworten geben,
    bevor jemand Fragen stellt,"
    Süddeutsche Zeitung, 24 October 2018.
    sueddeutsche.de/digital/
    google-discover-1.4181596.

2   Sebastian Klöß; Lukas Gentemann,
    "Das intelligente Zuhause: Smart Home 2020.
    Ein Bitkom-Studienbericht," September 2020.
    bitkom.org/sites/default/files/2020-09/
    200922_studienbericht_smart-home.pdf.

3   Benedikt Plass-Fleßenkämper; Manuel Bauer,
    "Alexa-Panne: Amazon Echo bestellt
    Puppenhäuser," *Computerbild,* 9 January 2017.
    computerbild.de/artikel/cb-News-Internet-
    Alexa-Panne-Amazon-Echo-Puppenhaeuser-
    17145863.html.

4   Olaf Kolbrück, "Künstliche Intelligenz: Pleiten,
    Pech und Pannen," *Etailment,* 16 December
    2019. etailment.de/news/stories/KI-Pannen-
    Adidas-Alexa-22386.

5   For a critical perspective, see Florian Rötzer,
    *Sein und Wohnen. Philosophische Streifzüge
    zur Geschichte und Bedeutung des Wohnens,*
    Frankfurt/Main, 2020. p. 9.

6   Oliver Herwig, *Universal Design. Lösungen für
    einen barrierefreien Alltag,* Basel, 2008.
    degruyter.com/document/doi/10.1515/
    9783034609678/html.

7   Jared Spataro, "2 years of digital transformation
    in 2 months," *Microsoft,* 30 April 2020.
    microsoft.com/en-us/microsoft-365/
    blog/2020/04/30/2-years-digital-
    transformation-2-months/.

8   ostblog.org/2013/04/kommunismus-ist-sowjet
    macht-plus-elektrifizierung-des-ganzen-landes/.

9   World Urbanization Prospects: 2018 Revision:
    Urban population (% of total population).
    United Nations Population Division.
    data.worldbank.org/indicator/SP.URB.TOTL.IN.ZS.

10 See Arne Holst, "Number of IoT connected
    devices worldwide 2019 – 2030," *Statista,* 20
    January 2021. statista.com/statistics/1194682/
    iot-connected-devices-vertically/.

11 See ourworldindata.org/world-population-
    growth; data.worldbank.org/indicator/sp.pop.
    grow.

12 Raymond Loewy, *Never Leave Well Enough
    Alone* (1951), Baltimore, 2002.

Home Smart Home:
Housing Glossary 2.0

157

The world is changing. And fast. The smart home has its own techno-language. Here is a brief, incomplete overview from the year 2022.

1234 Evidently the favorite >*Password* for PCs, >*Mobile Devices*, and more.

12345 Evidently the second favorite >*Password* for PCs, >*Mobile Devices*, and more.

24/7 Reachable around-the-clock. True for >*Internet* services and many of our contemporaries (>*Nerd*).

3D PRINTER Device for plotting three-dimensional objects on the basis of >*Data*. Abolishes the opposition between producers and users. Perfect for replacement parts in remote regions of the world, and perhaps one day for elements of domestic furnishing. Component of the >*Factory 4.0* and the >*IoT*.

5G Mobile communications standard for massive >*Data* quantities. Could replace private >*Router* and >*WLAN*.

ACCESS Admittance to the >*Internet*. For many, synonymous with happiness, since >*Networking* ensures social participation (>*Social Networking*).

ACCESS RIGHTS Determines who can do what with >*Programs* and >*Networks*. Primarily a >*Service* performed by >*Administrators*.

ACCOUNT A personal account for >*Users* in the >*Platform Economy*. The basis for using the >*Functions* of the >*Internet*.

ADMIN(ISTRATOR) De facto master of a Computer or >*Network*, establishes >*Access* Rights to >*Programs* (>*Functions*). In constant danger of being Hacked, and hence a potential >*Security* risk.

ADVERTISING A component of the business model of the >*Platform Economy*, >*Users* "pay" with their >*Data* for "cost-free" contents (>*Cookies*).

AI Artificial intelligence. A euphemistic designation for more-or-less well-programmed >*Algorithms* that draw on past quantities of data and profiles and require continuous >*Updates* in order to ensure the greater or lesser >*Security* of >*Data*.

AIRBNB Digital version of the classical bed & breakfast; has not only altered the way we go on vacation (as natives among natives, ensconced in ordinary homes, in the middle of town), but has also compelled some tourism destinations to issue restrictions on transforming apartments into rentable space. Part of the digital >*Platform Economy* (>*Update*).

ALEXA Artificial intelligence (>*AI*) or digital >*Assistant* of >*Amazon*, attached to the physical devices Amazon Echo, Echo Dot, and the Fire TV Stick. An element of the >*Smart Home*. For many, the legitimate successor to the hi-fi system and TV remote, with convenient >*Voice Control* and a function for Internet orders. For critics, a method of room surveillance and a portal providing access to user desires (>*User*). Competitors are Cortana (Microsoft), Siri (Apple), and so on.

ALGORITHM Logical sequence of commands that segments a problem into small steps in search of a solution. A component of >*AI* and hence of the >*Smart Home*.

ALLOTMENT GARDEN

(SCHREBERGARTEN) Small garden plot in a German city, used for recreation and to raise fruit, flowers, and vegetables. Formerly typical of the petite bourgeois, and feared for its strict ordinances. Meanwhile quite fashionable among young families. (>*Urban Gardening*).

AMAZON Internet retailer, founded in 1996 by Jeff Bezos, with headquarters in Seattle. One of the Big 5 (>*GAFAM*: Google, Apple, Facebook, Amazon, Microsoft). For many, a convenient (>*Convenience*) option for shopping around-the-clock (>*24/7*). Prime customers pay nothing for delivery, and have access to a comprehensive video-on-demand >*Streaming* platform. Some regard Amazon as causing the demise of small, owner-operated urban businesses and shops, and as a behemoth that crushes unionization and promotes unfair competition through a variety of tax avoidance strategies (oligopoly).

APP Abbreviation for application, a program that runs on a >*Mobile Device* and is decisive for >*Convenience*.

ASSISTANT Refers to digital entities which for the most part play a helpful support role (>*AI*).

AUGMENTED REALITY Superimposition onto the surroundings of artificial elements which behave >*Interactively* within space and with >*Users*. A common source of diversion.

BACKUP COPY Second version of important data, generally stored on an external hard drive or stick. Often a last resort following a >*Crash*.

BATTERY Energy supply for >*Mobile devices*. Usually with an operating time that is too short.

BETA TESTER In most cases, the involuntary >*User* of the newest version of a software (>*Update*) that is >*Downloaded* via the Internet after a >*Login*. Promises greater >*Security* and smoother >*Function*(ing) and/or >*Convenience*.

BIG DATA Basis of the >*Platform Economy*. User data is compiled from the most diverse sources. Added more recently are masses of machine data from the >*IoT*. It is only this gargantuan database that allows >*Algorithms* and >*AI* to pick out patterns from among aggregate data, generating unfamiliar linkages and testing new business models. Via >*WLAN* and >*5G*, the >*Smart Home* is a component of such >*Data* analysis.

BINGE-WATCHING Marathon viewing of TV series late into the night. An opportunity to see all of the episodes from a season in a single sitting, ideally on a sofa or in bed, and of >*Sharing* the experience with many >*Friends*.

BLUETOOTH Wireless device connection between mobile devices or between mobile devices and stationary devices such as printers, etc. The younger brother of the ubiquitous >*WLAN*.

BOX-SPRING (BED) Type of bed construction originating in the United States. Sleep experts and many senior citizens swear by the enhanced >*Comfort* of this classic, a box with springs, in other words: an inner-spring mattress and >*Topper*.

BROADBAND (INTERNET ACCESS) >*Internet* connection offering a higher >*Data* transmission rate. Makes living and working in the countryside possible.

CHARGING CABLE Connects >*Mobile devices* with a power supply. A kind of superior >*Battery*.

CLOUD Metaphorical designation for the >*Internet* and its capacity to store >*Data* somewhere other than a personal device.

COCOONING Encapsulation in one's own apartment, at times a voluntary withdrawal from the world (>*Nerd*).

COLIVING Digital >*Update* of the classic >*Residential Community*. Unlike the latter, not associated with periods of education and training. Generally featuring enhanced >*Comfort* and better furnishings. Central here are shared facilities such as the living kitchen; in some communities, each private room has its own bathroom.

COMFORT Key concept for the >*Smart Home*. According to a representative survey, 72% of >*Users* expect "greater comfort and quality of life" (>*Convenience*).

COMMON ROOMS The heart of every home, where people encounter one another in real space. Especially favored in Coworking and Coliving.

COMPATIBILITY Guarantees that >*Operating Systems* are able to communicate with >*Programs* and >*Mobile Devices* from the most diverse manufacturers.

CONVENIENCE Term meaning comfort and service. Earlier referred to as "Just like Mom's."

CONTENT More-or-less worthwhile content for which >*Users* pay, albeit often only with their >*Data*.

COOKIES Tiny data packets that are loaded by a >*Server* onto a Computer or Cell Phone during the use of electronic services >*Program*, and which make a >*User* identifiable. Basis of the >*Advertising*-financed >*Platform Economy* and of government surveillance.

COUCH SURFING Overnight stays with friends or people known only through digital platforms (>*Social Media*). Noncommercial form of >*Airbnb*.

COWORKING Rented workplace shared by like-minded people, who are generally strangers prior to the arrangement. Shared office with >*Internet*, >*WLAN*, and optional services. Not a classical office, but instead a temporary partnership, used preferentially by Digital Nomads and people who require little more than a >*Notebook* and good Reception (of data, not an area staffed by a receptionist).

CRASH Breakdown of >*Programs* and Computers, generally through imprecise >*Programming*, >*User* error, and more rarely through >*Hacker* attacks. Accompanied by the danger that >*Data* is lost. Those prioritizing >*Security* create a >*Security* Backup Copy.

DATA The preferred way of paying for the seemingly free services of the >*Platform Economy*: through the disclosure of one's own habits, preferences, and desires. Closely associated with smooth >*Access* to the >*Internet*.

DATA PROTECTION A big thing in Europe, often voluntarily annulled through the daily activities of the >*User*, >*Cookies*.

DELIVERY SERVICES
(FOODORA, LIEFERANDO AND CO.)
They come to the rescue during attacks of appetite in the office, the >*Home Office*, or in the >*Coworking* workplace. The courier is generally a poorly paid individual on an >*E-Bike*. Designed for the >*Convenience* of users.

DIGITAL CONCIERGE Internet successor to the all-knowing concierge, traditionally the soul of an apartment building in France or the US: digital >*Access* control to one's own apartment thanks to a >*Password*, >*RFID*, or digital keyring. A component of comprehensive around-the-clock >*24/7* >*Service* provision.

DIGITAL NOMADS Those who renounce the maintenance of an apartment, a form of reduction (>*Couch Surfing*).

DISPLAY SCREEN Somewhat antiquated name for a monitor (>*TV*).

DOCKING STATION Links portable devices, for example with a hi-fi device, for the most part superseded by WLAN.

DOLBY SURROUND Sound system with multiple coordinated channels that promise good sound quality.

DOWNLOADS Reception of >*Data* on a PC, and a term often used in connection with download speed. Important for >*Streaming* platforms such as >*Netflix*, which offer downloadable Videos on demand.

DRONES Autonomous miniature helicopters which may become vitally important for >*Delivery Services* in the future.

EARLY ADOPTER Avant-gardist with a tendency toward technical innovation (>*Nerd*).

E-BIKE Bicycle with electric auxiliary propulsion, successor to the Moped; minimizes age differences.

FACEBOOK >*Social Network* that has lost its fashionable status.

FACTORY 4.0 The >*Smart* factory that links tools and >*Data* in the >*IoT*.

FEEDBACK Transmission of evaluative or corrective information about a Control source and its implementation, or with a >*User* (>*Interactive*).

FLAT RATE A one-time payment. Often by subscription. Important for extensive >*Downloads* from the >*Internet*.

FOLLOWER The only >*Friends* who can actually be purchased. Aside from house pets.

FRIEND For the most part a physically existing person, but sometimes only a >*Follower*.

FUNCTION Their scope defines the performance capacity of >*Programs*. Decisive criterion: >*Convenience*.

GADGET Inconsequential plaything, generally free of charge. Extra feature for mobile devices.

GAFAM Acronym for the five leading firms of the >*Platform Economy*: Google, Apple, Facebook, Amazon, and Microsoft.

GESTURE CONTROL In conjunction with >*Voice Control*, a comfortable >*Convenience* form of control in the >*Smart Home*.

HACKER Safecracker of the digital age, dreaded by all who are concerned with their >*Security* (Cell Phone, >*Password*).

HOME OFFICE Office located within one's own four walls. Often involuntarily.

HOMESCHOOLING Instruction undertaken at home when school is canceled due to the pandemic. Often re-sults in overburdened parents.

HOUSING 4.0 Modern >*Residential Communities*. Most use elements of the >*Smart Home*.

HYGGE More than comfy or homey. Danish for "snug," "intimate," "comfortable," "small but nice," "twee." >*Wikipedia* says: "used by the Danes themselves as a national stereotype."

INNOVATION The aggregate of many >*Updates*.

INSTAGRAM Social network for sharing and commenting on images. Decisive for >*Follower*(s) and >*Likes*.

INTERACTIVE Preferred mode of the >*Smart Home*. It responds to con-trol (mostly, at least) and pro-vides the >*User* with >*Feedback*.

INTERFACE Input device, generally a graphic >*User Interface*.

INTERNET Connected to most of the PCs on the planet. Among the greatest cultural achievements of humanity. Formerly a beacon of democracy and freedom, meanwhile misused for purposes of >*24/7* surveillance.

IOT The Internet of Things networks formerly independent devices (>*Stand-Alone*) for a >*Smart Home*.

IPAD Large Cell Phone, ideal for film evenings (>*Binge*-Watching).

KING-SIZED Augmentation of the 140-centime-ter >*Queen-sized* bed. A full two meters in width.

LED Light-emitting diode (actually a semiconductor) designed to reduce energy use compared with old-style lightbulbs. Which it does. The result, however, is often nullified by the burning of more lamps for longer periods of time. Offers excellent controllability, and meanwhile outstanding color as well (>*OLED*).

LIFE HACK >*Wikipedia*: "A life hack is any trick, shortcut, skill, or novelty method that increases productivity and efficiency, in all walks of life." Clever shortcut, ingenious simplification found on the >*Internet*.

LIKES Expression of approval for other people's posts on >*Social Platforms*; the effective currency among networked people, together with the number of >*Followers*.

LOGIN Initiates >*Programs* after a >*Password* has been entered.

MASTER BEDROOM US-American term for the main bedroom of a residence. Implies the presence of additional children's or guest bedrooms. The term has recently come under heavy criticism for its racist and sexist implications.

MOBILE DEVICE Collective Name for Cell Phone, >*iPad*, or >*Notebook*. Controlled by graphic user interfaces.

NERD Affectionate or at times pejorative term for mostly (young) men (rarely women) who are high achievers in their (usually technical) areas of specialization and >*Programs*, and lack a degree of practical wisdom (>*Early Adopter*). Often experts in the >*Smart Home*.

NETFLIX >*Streaming* provider of films and television series that has sup-planted the immobile television in many households. Makes possible the delayed individual consumption of entire seasons in a single sitting (>*Binge-Watching*).

NETWORKING Network of relationships and basic pattern of modern society, perfected on the

>*Internet* and through >*Social Networks*.

NOTEBOOK Or laptop: portable PC, in contradistinction to a desktop PC.

OLED The organic light-emitting diode is ideal for area lighting, and is used for many display screens on >*Mobile Devices*. A supplement to the >*LED*.

ONLINE SHOPPING Modern form of shopping(>*24/7*).

OPERATING SYSTEM Basic >*Program* for running digital devices.

PACKSTATION In Germany, a colossal external mailbox for packages and other deliveries that might otherwise wind up with neighbors or be returned to senders.

PASSWORD Personal identification that provides minimal protection against unauthorized access to >*Accounts*, >*Social Networks*, >*Online* Shopping and Banking. The problem: >*1234* is easy to remember, everything else easy to forget. Throws a spotlight on the topic of >*Security*.

PLATFORM ECONOMY Form of organization on the Internet through which individual enterprises dominate entire business sectors (oligopoly), with a negative impact on competitiveness. Often (>*Convenient)* for users.

POSTING >*Sharing*.

POWER SOCKET Analog form of the >*Battery*. Together with the extension cord, a necessary evil.

PROGRAM Computer language, and hence the basis for >*AI*, the >*Smart Home*, the >*Internet*, and the rest of the digital world.

PROJECTOR Successor to the television. Converts a white wall with armchair and sofa into a virtual home cinema (>*Dolby Surround*).

QUEEN-SIZED The 140-centimeter bed, replaced meanwhile by the two-meter-wide >*King-Sized* bed.

REMOTE The good old remote control in a digital guise. Makes it possible to control the >*Functions* of the >*Smart Home* from anywhere. Which is >*Convenient*, but perhaps also a question of >*Security*.

RESIDENTIAL COMMUNITY An apartment shared by a number of unrelated individuals; known earlier as a student apartment.

RFID Radio Frequency Identification. Radio chip and devices which convey your location, among other things.

ROBOT VACUUM CLEANER Autonomous vacuum cleaner that can be activated >*24/7*.

ROUTER Telephone switchboard for your own four walls. Source of >*WLAN*, and of outbursts of despair when it breaks down.

SEARCH ENGINE Virtual catalog of the >*Internet*, makes it possible to locate dispersed >*Content*.

SECURITY Perceived or actual protection from a (presumed) threat. Dealt with for the most part by technical means >*Password*, >*Video Surveillance*.

SERVER Data farms, often located in remote parts of the world. Supposedly "servants"!—Perceived as the masters of the >*Internet*, which make >*Programs* available for >*Download*, which in turn make Video-On-Demand and various service providers of the >*Platform Economy* possible.

SERVICE >*Convenience*

SERVICED APARTMENTS A hybrid of hotel and apartment that offers >*Convenience* and a high degree of individuality.

SHARING A way of making >*Internet* content available to others.

SLEEP ANALYZER Device that monitors the depth and duration of sleep, can be helpful in optimizing sleep quality.

SMART HOME Refers to the networked residence and its devices, which permit external surveillance and control.

SMART SWITCH "Intelligent" light switch that makes lighting management possible (dimming, color changes, scenarios, etc.), making it a part of the >*IoT*, and requiring a "smart bulb" as a companion piece.

SOCIAL NETWORK / SOCIAL MEDIA Part of the >*Platform Economy* of the >*Internet*, based on >*Networking* between people; becomes a daily task of the >*User* through >*Likes* and >*Followers*, as well as content >*Sharing*.

STAND-ALONE Autonomous isolated applications, the converse of >*Networking*. Out of fashion.

STREAMING Successor of the video library and the >*TV* program: videos and other content are no longer stored on a hard drive, but can instead be called up >*24/7*.

THREAD Trendy wireless standard, evidently highly-efficient in battery use, based on the protocol IPv6. Competitors include Zigbee and Z-Wave.

TOPPER Additional top layer for a mattress. Promises enhanced >*Comfort*.

TV Outdated, associated with linear television.

UPDATE Part of the >*Platform Economy* of the >*Internet*, which promises the best of all possible worlds through the most up-to-date version of a software program. Generally obligatory for the >*User* to ensure a certain standard of >*Security*.

URBAN GARDENING Horticulture as practiced in cities, often in impossible locations. Small gardens cultivated with much devotion, younger sister of the old >*Allotment Garden*, which is currently enjoying a renaissance.

USER The ordinary user of technical devices and services. Users desire >*Convenience*, and are often concerned about the >*Security* of their >*Data* (>*Update*).

USER INTERFACE >*Interactive* graphic surface of >*Mobile Devices*, which makes possible the Control of the >*Smart Home*, meanwhile supplemented by >*Voice Control* and >*Gesture Control*.

VIDEO SURVEILLANCE Generally begins already in the nursery. Potentially easy to Hack. Provides a sense of >*Security*.

VIRTUAL For the older generation, still the opposite of analog, meanwhile however no longer clearly distinguishable from real surroundings as a consequence of forms of >*Augmented Reality*.

VOICE CONTROL Together with >*Gesture Control*, a welcome >*Convenience*. A form of Control of the >*Smart Home*.

VR Virtual Reality, artificial worlds into which users can become submerged via >*Gadgets*; big sister of >*Augmented Reality*.

WEB >*Internet*.

WI-FI Colloquially referred to as a wireless network. Actually the corporate name of >*WLAN* devices operating on the basis of IEEE 802.11 standards. Since no one can remember that, a branding consultant came up with a memorable artificial name that echoes the term hi-fi.

WIKIPEDIA Digital advance over Brockhaus & Co, eliminates mountains of books, which age quickly. Compiled global knowledge. Advantage: anyone can contribute. Disadvantage: anyone can contribute.

WLAN Wireless data transmission in your own apartment or in public locations. Generally protected by a >*Password*.

Housing Glossary 2.0

Who has residential property in Europe?

Romania
95,8 %

Poland
84,2 %

Spain
76,2 %

United Kingdom
65,2 %

France
65,1 %

Austria
55,2 %

Germany
51,1 %

Switzerland
42,5 %

Housing Glossary 2.0

Appendix

ACKNOWLEDGMENTS

The book updates a series of articles which originally appeared in the Süddeutsche Zeitung as the series "Wie wir wohnen" (How We Live); my thanks in particular to Marianne Körber and Andreas Remien and also to the team at Birkhäuser Verlag, especially Dr. Ulrich Schmidt, Ulrike Ruh, Baharak Tajbakhsh, and Katharina Kulke, and to the designers of the "Studio für Gestaltung" (Cologne/Berlin). Without COR's support, Home Smart Home would never have been published. Thank you, Leo Lübke.

SOURCES

ALLGEMEINE HOTEL- UND GASTRONOMIE-ZEITUNG
ahgz.de/hoteldesign/news/wir-werden-sehr-viel-flexibler-leben-264126.

AMK
Arbeitsgemeinschaft Die Moderne Küche e.V. (AMK): *Küchentrends 2021.* AMK, 4.2.21.
amk.de/pressemeldung/kuechentrends-2021/.

ARD/ZDF
ard-zdf-onlinestudie.de/files/2020/0920_Beisch_Schaefer.pdf.

ÄRZTEBLATT
Gross, Werner:
"Messie-Syndrom: Löcher in der Seele stopfen."
PP 1, September 2002, p. 419.

AUSTRIA REAL GMBH
justimmo-websites.s3.eu-central-1.amazonaws.com/551d18b8cb24ed0cccea76b03d73cefde05cd76a/source.

BAYERISCHE VERFASSUNG
bayerische-verfassung.de/artikel-151-bis-177/#Art_161.

BITKOM
Klöß, Sebastian; Gentemann, Lukas:
"Das intelligente Zuhause: Smart Home 2020."
Ein Bitkom-Studienbericht, September 2020.

BUNDESINSTITUT FÜR BEVÖLKERUNGSFORSCHUNG
bib.bund.de/DE/Service/Presse/2013/2013-07-Pro-Kopf-Wohnflaeche-erreicht-mit-45-m2-neuen-Hoechstwert.html.

BUNDESZENTRALE FÜR POLITISCHE BILDUNG
Hasse, Jürgen:
Was bedeutet es, zu wohnen? Bundeszentrale für Politische Bildung, 15.6.2018.

BUNDESBAUBLATT
bundesbaublatt.de/artikel/bbb_Klein_kleiner_mikro_1987397.html.

BUNDESINSTITUT FÜR BAU-, STADT- UND RAUMFORSCHUNG
bbsr.bund.de/BBSR/DE/FP/ReFo/Staedtebau/2017/kleingaerten/03-ergebnisse.html.

BUNDESMINISTERIUM FÜR ERNÄHRUNG UND LANDWIRTSCHAFT
ernaehrungsvorsorge.de/private-vorsorge/notvorrat/vorratskalkulator/.

BUNDESVERBAND DIGITALE WIRTSCHAFT (BVDW) E.V.
Study: Mehrheit der deutschen Angestellten wünscht sich wegen des Corona-Virus Home-Office. Mehrzahl der Arbeitgeber wäre dazu technisch in der Lage.

BUSINESS INSIDER
Rudnick, Hendrikje:
"World wide study by Stepstone: 90 Prozent der Arbeitnehmer wollen weiterhin mobil arbeiten."
Business Insider, 31.3.2021.

COMPUTERBILD
Plass-Fleßenkämper, Benedikt; Bauer, Manuel:
"Alexa-Panne: Amazon Echo bestellt Puppenhäuser."
Computerbild, 9.1.2017.

ETAINMENT
Kolbrück, Olaf:
"Künstliche Intelligenz: Pleiten, Pech und Pannen."
Etailment, 16.12.2019. etailment.de/news/stories/KI-Pannen-Adidas-Alexa-22386.

FOCUS
Farwer, Lukas:
"Lebensdauer einer Küche – alle Infos zur Haltbarkeit." *Focus online,* 30.11.2017.

FRANKFURTER ALLGEMEINE ZEITUNG
Dettweiler, Marco:
"Heiß und trendig. So sieht die moderne Küche aus. Corona schickt die Menschen zurück an den Herd. Das hat zur Folge, dass viele ihre Küche neu einrichten. Die Nachfrage nach Geräten ist zurzeit enorm. Falls sie noch nicht bestellt haben: Wir helfen und zeigen Ihnen, was momentan in der Küche so angesagt ist." *Frankfurter Allgemeine Zeitung,* 10.5.2021.
Fehr, Mark:
"Fünf ernüchternde Fakten zum Mieten, Kaufen und Wohnen. Vier Millionen Deutsche träumen von einem Eigenheim. Doch ein Blick auf die nackten Zahlen zeigt, das der Traum sich für viele nicht erfül-

len wird. Ein kleiner Trost: Mieten hat auch Vorteile."
Frankfurter Allgemeine Zeitung, 17.5.2021.

Holzer, Boris:
"Die Logik des guten Geschmacks. Intellektuelle schauen Serien und hören Rap. Aber elitär muss es sein." *Frankfurter Allgemeine Sonntagszeitung*, 1.8.2021.

Maak, Niklas:
"Häuser für eine andere Welt. In der Schweiz revolutionieren junge Büros wie Duplex Architekten mit aufsehenerregenden Wohnexperimenten unsere Vorstellung von der Zukunft der Stadt. Wie könnte die aussehen?" *Frankfurter Allgemeine Zeitung*, 21.6.2021.

Rampe Henrik:
"WG für Berufstätige: Mehr als ein Zweckbündnis. Nicht nur Studis, auch immer mehr Menschen jenseits der dreißig ziehen in WGs. Was treibt Professorinnen und Familienväter dazu, sich mit anderen Kühlschrank und Putzdienst zu teilen?"
Frankfurter Allgemeine Zeitung, 9.6.2021.

"Sehnsucht nach dem Büro." Meldung. Frankfurter Allgemeine Zeitung, 10.4.2021, p. C1. Their reference to survey of the job portal "Stepstone."

"So viel geht in Großstädten vom Gehalt für die Miete drauf. Neue Studie. Jeder achte deutsche Großstadthaushalt gibt mehr als die Hälfte seines Einkommens für die Miete aus. Doch die Lage hat sich zuletzt gebessert." *Frankfurter Allgemeine Zeitung*, 15.6.2021.

GLOBENEWSWIRE
globenewswire.com/en/news-release/2014/01/30/924112/0/en/New-Report-on-Luxury-Buying-Spotlights-Cities-and-Customer-Segments.html.

HANNOVERSCHE ALLGEMEINE ZEITUNG
Fröhlich, Sonja:
"Warum Erwachsene lieber in eine WG ziehen."
Hannoversche Allgemeine Zeitung, 3.4.2016.

HANS-BÖCKLER-STIFTUNG
boeckler.de/de/boeckler-impuls-unbezahlbare-mieten-4100.htm.

INSTYLE
InStyle, (2018):
"Wer seine Wohnung früh weihnachtlich dekoriert, ist glücklicher."

PROF. DR. STEFAN KOFNER
Kofner, Stefan:
Übers Wohnen.
hogareal.de/html/ubers_wohnen.html.

KONRAD-ADENAUER-STIFTUNG
Schneider, Hans Dietmar; Hoffmann, Elisabeth:
Familienförderung durch Wohneigentum. Kindern ein Zuhause geben. Konrad-Adenauer-Stiftung e. V., Sankt Augustin/Berlin, 2018.

MALISA STIFTUNG
"Weibliche Selbstinszenierung in den neuen Medien." Results of a series of studies presented by MaLisa Foundation, January 2019.

MICROSOFT
Spataro, Jared:
"2 years of digital transformation in 2 months."
Microsoft, 30.4.2020.

MKG HAMBURG
mkg-hamburg.de/de/ausstellungen/archiv/2021/together.html.

NDR
ndr.de/kultur/Revival-der-Zimmerpflanzen, zimmerpflanzen168.html.
ndr.de/ratgeber/garten/zimmerpflanzen/Bogenhanf-Robuste-Zimmerpflanze-im-Retro-Look,bogenhanf102.html.

NTV
ntv, 13.12.
"Album ohne Voankündigung: Beyoncé landet Coup." ntv, 13.12.2013

SPARKASSE MAINZ
Hörner, Daniel:
"So wohnen wir." Sparkasse Mainz, 26.11.2019

STATISTA
Ahrens Sandra:
"Wie häufig wird in Ihrem Haushalt gekocht?" Survey on the frequency of cooking in Germany 2021, conducted among around 1,000 respondents. Statista, 20.5.2021.

Graefe, Lena:
"Für welche Zwecke nutzt Ihr Unternehmen Serviced Apartments? Umfrage unter Unternehmen weltweit zur Nutzung von Serviced Apartments bis 2019." *Statista,* 7.1.2021.

Graefe, Lena:
"Statistiken zum Reiseverhalten der Deutschen."
Statista, 12.7.21.

Hohmann, M.:
"Statistiken zu Küchenmöbeln in Deutschland."
Statista, 9.06.2021.

Hohmann, M.:
"Umsatz der deutschen Küchenindustrie in den Jahren 2008 bis 2020." *Statista*, 16.4.2021.

Holst, Arne:
"Number of IoT connected devices worldwide 2019 – 2030." *Statista*, 20.1.2021.

Statista Research Department:
"Wohneigentumsquote in ausgewählten Ländern Europas 2019." *Statista*, 15.12.2020.

Statista Research Department:
"Aussagen zum Stellenwert der Küche in der Wohnung." *Statista*, 30.8.2008.

STIFTUNG WARENTEST
"Selfstorage. So schaffen Sie schnell mal Platz."
Stiftung Warentest, 10.9.2014.

SÜDDEUTSCHE ZEITUNG
Hurtz, Simon:
"Google will Antworten geben, bevor jemand Fragen stellt." *Süddeutsche Zeitung*, 24.10.2018.

Matzig, Gerhard:
"Wohnen: Über Garagen und was darin zu finden ist." *Süddeutsche Zeitung*, 2.4.2021.

Neidhart, Christoph:
"Warum Japaner Autos mieten – und nirgends damit hinfahren." *Süddeutsche Zeitung*, 10.7.2019.

"Verlängertes Wohnzimmer. Eine neue Service-Idee erobert deutsche Metropolen. Mit Miet-Boxen zur Einlagerung von Hausrat, Hobby-Ausrüstung, Umzugsgut oder Archivmaterialien erzielen clevere Anbieter schon heute Millionenumsätze."
Süddeutsche Zeitung, 10.5.2020.

SWR
Haungs, Julia:
"Radikal anders wohnen – Leben in Bauhaus-Architektur." *SWR2*, 29.6.2020.

TAZ
Dribbusch, Barbara; Beucker, Pascal:
"Rückzug aufs Hochbett. Die Mietpreise in den Ballungszentren steigen. Deshalb drängen sich dort immer mehr Familien in einer zu kleinen Wohnung."
taz, 11.6.2014.

Palmer, Georgia:
"Die Revolte der neuen Dienstboten. FahrerInnen unter Druck, Profite streichen andere ein. Es regt sich Widerstand gegen die Arbeitsbedingungen bei Lieferdiensten wie Foodora." *taz*, 22.7.2017.

TOPHOTEL
tophotel.de/auswirkungen-der-krise-und-zukunfts prognosemarktreport-serviced-apartments-2021-veroeffentlicht-97262/

UNITED NATIONS POPULATION DIVISION
World Urbanization Prospects:
2018 Revision: Urban population (% of total population). United Nations Population Division.

UNIVERSITÄT HOHENHEIM
Elsner, Dorothea:
"Macht Wohneigentum glücklich?"
Study of the University Hohenheim, 5.5.2015.

VISIT DENMARK
visitdenmark.de/daenemark/erlebnisse/hygge.

DIE WELT
Bude, Heinz:
"Prolegomena zu einer Soziologie der Party."
Welt, 23.11.2015.

WORLDBANK
worldbank.org/indicator/sp.pop.grow.

DIE ZEIT
Augustin, Kersten; Friedrichs, Julia:
"Wird erledigt. Ein Mietshaus in Berlin. Servicekräfte huschen rein und raus. Hier erzählen sie, was sie wirklich von ihren Jobs und ihren Auftraggebern halten." *Die Zeit*, 3.11.2016.

BIBLIOGRAPHY

Benjamin, Walter:
The Arcades Project.
Cambridge, MA, 2002.

Dell, Christopher:
Ware: Wohnen. Politik. Ökonomie.
Städtebau. Berlin, 2013.

Espedal, Tomas:
Biografie, Tagebuch, Briefe.
Berlin, 2017.

Faller, Peter:
Der Wohngrundriss. Untersuchung im Auftrag der
Wüstenrot Stiftung. Munich, 2002.

Fischer, Volker; Hamilton, Anne eds.:
Theorien der Gestaltung. Grundalgentexte zum
Design. Vol. 1. Frankfurt am Main, 1999.

Grunwald, Armin; Hartlieb, Justus von, eds.:
Ist Technik die Zukunft der menschlichen Natur?
Hannover, 2012.

Häußermann, Hartmut; Siebel, Walter:
Soziologie des Wohnens. Eine Einführung in Wandel
und Ausdifferenzierung des Wohnens. Munich, 1996.

Herwig, Oliver:
Universal Design. Lösungen für
einen barrierefreien Alltag. Basel, 2008.
degruyter.com/document/
doi/10.1515/9783034609678/html.

Hubeli, Ernst:
Die neue Krise der Städte. Zur Wohnungsfrage
im 21. Jahrhundert. Zurich, 2020.

Küstenmacher, Werner; Seiwert, Lothar J.:
Simplify your Life. Einfacher und glücklicher leben.
Frankfurt am Main, 2004.

Lampugnani, Vittorio Magnago:
Die Stadt im 20. Jahrhundert. Visionen,
Entwürfe, Gebautes. Berlin, 2010.

Loos, Adolf:
"Die moderne Siedlung," 1926. In: Loos, Adolf:
Sämtliche Schriften in zwei Bänden – Vol. 1,
edited by Franz Glück, Wien, 1962, p. 402 – 428.
Quoted from: Wikisource. de.wikisource.org/wiki/
Die_moderne_Siedlung#Anmerkungen_des_
Herausgebers.

Montenegro, Riccardo:
"Enzyklopädie der Wohnkultur. Von der Antike bis
zur Gegenwart." Cologne, 1997.

Müller-Doohm, Stefan
Die kulturelle Kodierung des Schlafens oder: Wovon
das Schlafzimmer ein Zeichen ist, in: *Soziale Welt, 47,*
no. 1 (1996): p. 110 – 122.
uol.de/stefan-mueller-doohm/publikationen.

Müller-Doohm, Stefan; Jung, Thomas:
"Kultur und Natur im Schlafraum," in: Stefan
Müller-Doohm und Klaus Neumann-Braun, eds.:
Kulturinszenierungen, Frankfurt a. M., 1995,
pp. 239 – 262.

Müller-Doohm, Stefan;
Jung, Thomas, Vogt, Ludgera:
"Wovon das Schlafzimmer ein Zeichen ist. Text- und
Bildanalysen von Schlafraumkultur im Werbeme-
dium," in: Hans A. Hartmann and Rolf Haubl, eds.:
Bilderflut und Sprachmagie. Fallstudien zur Kultur
der Werbung, Opladen, 1992, pp. 245 – 266.

Riley, Terence:
The Un-Private House.
Museum of Modern Art,
New York City, 1999.

Rötzer, Florian:
Sein und Wohnen. Philosophische Streifzüge zur
Geschichte und Bedeutung des Wohnens.
Frankfurt/Main, 2020.

Schmidt, Eric; Cohen, Jared:
Die Vernetzung der Welt. Ein Blick in unsere Zukunft.
Hamburg, 2013.

Schütte-Lihotzky, Margarete:
"Rationalisierung im Haushalt," 1926. In:
Fischer, Volker; Hamilton, Anne, eds.:
Theorien der Gestaltung. Grundalgentexte zum
Design. Vol. 1. Frankfurt am Main, 1999. pp. 169 – 172.
First published in: *Das Neue Frankfurt* 5/1926/27.

Seidel, Florian:
New small apartments.
Köln, 2008.

Together! Die Neue Architektur der Gemeinschaft:
Edited by Mateo Kries, Mathias Müller, Daniel Niggli,
Andreas Ruby, Ilka Ruby. Vitra Design Museum, Weil
am Rhein, 2017.

Trentmann, Frank:
*Herrschaft der Dinge. Die Geschichte des Konsums
vom 15. Jahrhundert bis heute.* Munich, 2016.

Vogel, Hans-Jochen:
*Mehr Gerechtigkeit!: Wir brauchen eine neue
Bodenordnung – nur dann wird auch Wohnen wieder
bezahlbar.* Freiburg im Breisgau, 2019.

CONTRIBUTIONS OLIVER HERWIG

"Mit Schirm, ohne Charme."
Süddeutsche Zeitung, 28.10.2016.

"Zelle, Grotte, Wellness-Tempel."
Süddeutsche Zeitung, 16.9.2016.

"Abschied von der guten Stube."
Süddeutsche Zeitung, 8.7.2016.

"Eigernordwand in Furnier. "
Süddeutsche Zeitung, 24.3.2017.

"Chaos im Kinderzimmer."
Süddeutsche Zeitung, 10./11.7.2021.
www.sueddeutsche.de/leben/chaos-im-
kinderzimmer-aufraeumen-erziehung-
1.5343984?reduced=true.

"Das Ende der Privatheit."
Süddeutsche Zeitung, 30.9.2016.

"Bettgeschichten."
Süddeutsche Zeitung, 23.12.2016.

"Draußen vor der Tür."
Süddeutsche Zeitung, 19.8.2016.

"Mit Kürbis und Hortensie
trotzen wir dem Chaos."
Neue Zürcher Zeitung, 26.9.2016.

"Freiheit im Untergrund."
Süddeutsche Zeitung, 11./12.1.2020.

"Keller und Dachboden werden edel."
Süddeutsche Zeitung, 29.7.2016.

"Ein schöner Schrein."
Süddeutsche Zeitung, 30.12.2016.

"Die Welt nach Corona.
Wer schützt das Home vor dem Office?"
Frankfurter Rundschau, 9.6.2020.

"Die Weißenhofsiedlung in Stuttgart."
Architare, 2020.

"Hotelification oder das leichte Leben."
Lifeathome, 13.11.2018.

"Sucht und Ordnung."
Lifeathome, 18.9.2018.

"Together!"
KAP Forum, 2021.

"Zusammenhalten. Die neue Architektur der
Gemeinschaft."
Interview.

"Ware Wohnen oder das wahre Wohnen:
Wem gehört die Stadt?"
Frankfurter Rundschau, 19.8.2020.

"Lob des Zwischenraums."
Transformational Buildings, 2021.

Translation from German into English: Ian Pepper
Copy editing: Patricia Kot
Project management: Baharak Tajbakhsh,
                                       Katharina Kulke
Production: Heike Strempel
Layout, cover design & typesetting: Studio für Gestaltung, Cologne,
                                       Chan Sperle
Illustrations: Studio für Gestaltung, Cologne,
                                       Chan Sperle, Dominik Kirgus
Infographics: Studio für Gestaltung, Cologne,
                                       Maja Grass
Paper: Amber Graphic 120 g/m²
Printing: Eberl & Koesel GmbH & Co. KG,
                                       Altusried-Krugzell

Library of Congress Control Number: 2022931507
Bibliographic information published by The German National Library lists this
the German National Library   publication in the Deutsche National-
                                      bibliografie; detailed bibliographic data
                                      are available on the Internet at
                                      http://dnb.dnb.de.
        ISBN   978-3-0356-2443-4
        e-ISBN (PDF)   978-3-0356-2449-6
        German Print-ISBN   978-3-0356-2442-7
©2022 Birkhäuser Verlag GmbH, Basel
P.O. Box 44, 4009 Basel, Switzerland
        Part of Walter de Gruyter GmbH,
        Berlin/Boston
9 8 7 6 5 4 3 2 1
www.birkhauser.com

With the friendly
support of: